Mourning God may be the single most important book I've read in the last decade. With pastoral tenderness and theological precision, Tiffany brilliantly and wholeheartedly reveals how our pain shapes our view of God. Her words have transformed me. I will never get over the significance of this book and the way it will guide a generation of Christians longing to process the heaviness of our times with honesty and without losing hope.

KAT ARMSTRONG, Bible teacher, author, and podcast host

In her excellent book *Mourning God*, Stein probes the hard questions many Christians hesitate to ask about grief. She charts a biblically sound path forward to a richer, stronger faith—one that sees the God who is, who loves with an undying love. A must-read for pastors and those desiring a deeper walk with God.

LYNN H. COHICK, PHD, Distinguished Professor of New Testament at Houston Christian University

In *Mourning God*, Tiffany Stein offers a brave reflection on grief, faith, and the seeming absence of God after the loss of her infant. With raw honesty and spiritual depth, she invites readers into a sacred journey of lament and longing. Her voice is that of a faithful companion for anyone navigating sorrow and searching for God in the silence.

SANDRA GLAHN, coauthor of *When Empty Arms Become a Heavy Burden*

Perhaps the most beautiful and bottomless theological project humans ever face is discovering the God who is and separating him from the God we imagine. Nothing aids that divination like suffering, and out of her own suffering Tiffany Stein has a deeply personal lesson for every person of faith. Because we all suffer, we need grace. Because we all misunderstand God, we need truth. Tiffany is a guide to help us find the God of grace and truth in a world of hurt. Listen to her.

RYAN SANDERS, commentary editor at *The Dallas Morning News* and author of *Unbelievable*

With searing honesty and hard-won faith, Tiffany Stein does what few dare to do: She names the secondary grief that comes when the God you thought you knew no longer fits in the categories you've constructed. She invites the reader into the metaphorical counseling room with God himself, refusing to settle for trite answers or spiritual bypassing. For anyone who has felt abandoned or disillusioned by God, *Mourning God* is theology forged in the furnace of real suffering. Read it when you're ready to ask your hard questions, and be prepared to let Tiffany Stein lead you to unflinching, yet hope-fueled, answers.

AUBREY SAMPSON, author of *What We Find in the Dark* and *The Louder Song*

Having the privilege of knowing Tiffany, I can confidently say that she doesn't just write about this topic; she lives it. Tiffany has not just intellectually learned about grief, suffering, and how to reorient her view God, she has applied it to her life and the lives of others. If you've ever struggled with your view of God, particularly amid pain, please read Tiffany's work. She writes with a shepherd's heart, a scholar's wisdom, and a deep conviction of the goodness of God.

TORIANO MAYO, lead pastor of The Well Austin Community Church

If loss or shattered dreams have sadly led to a loss of your God, this book is for you. Tiffany will gently take you by the hand and lead you through death and darkness back into the light and life of your Savior! She has walked this path and can show you the way.

LINDA DILLOW, author of *Hope for My Hurting Heart* and *Calm My Anxious Heart*

Why does God let good people (and especially his own children!) suffer? My wife, Alice, and I were with the Steins at the hospital where doctors had summoned them to say goodbye to their infant son, David. We bear witness that the Steins' personal traumatic journey began not only with the pain of losing their child but also with the arguably even greater pain of feeling abandoned by God. This is the refreshingly unique and powerfully credible perspective of *Mourning God*. Tiffany does not address the problem of pain emotionally, from the sterile heights of a philosopher, but biblically, from the tearstained depths of a broken heart. That means that she moves past shallow answers (which are short-lived and cheap) in favor of this deep wisdom (which is enduring and costly): "Ours is the God who comes near and mourns with us."

E. ANDREW McQUITTY, ThM, DMin, pastor and author of *Notes from the Valley*, *The Way to Brave*, *Hobo Pastors* (with Larry Parsley), and *Your Best Life Later*

I had the sacred privilege of walking closely with Tiffany and Jason through the brief but beautiful life of their son, David. His life and their faith have indelibly marked my own. *Mourning God* carries the hard-won wisdom of one who has wrestled honestly with God and found him faithful even in the dark. Tiffany writes with honesty, courage, and profound pastoral wisdom about grief, doubt, and the God who meets us in our deepest sorrow. This book will be a faithful companion for anyone struggling to trust the God they thought they knew and will serve as a gentle guide back to hope.

BARRY D. JONES, senior pastor of Irving Bible Church and author of *Dwell*

In Tiffany Stein's tender reflection on the death of her son, we encounter the God who not only stands sovereign over the depths but also, and crucially, remains lovingly with us there. To encounter such a God, as Stein recounts in this lovely book, is to experience the beginning of healing and hope, two things that those who find themselves in the depths fear they might never experience. May this book be a balm to your soul and a companion to you in the dark days and nights when you find yourself wrestling with God—and, by grace, finding your way back to life.

W. DAVID O. TAYLOR, associate professor of theology and culture at Fuller Theological Seminary and author of *Open and Unafraid* and *Prayers for the Pilgrimage*

Tiffany Stein had me at "death sucks." I am wary of those who glorify death (as if Jesus did not come to vanquish it) or pretend that grief and loss cannot disrupt a Christian's faith in God. This book does neither. Rather, it is as chock-full of vulnerable honesty about the tension of clinging to God after loss as it is of insightful Bible exposition and hope.

SHARIFA STEVENS, ThM, author of *When We Talk to God: Prayers and Poems for Black Women*

GRIEVING LOSS,

WRESTLING WITH GOD,

mourning GOD

AND FINDING YOUR WAY

BACK TO LIFE

TIFFANY STEIN

Published in alliance with Tyndale House Publishers

NavPress.com

Mourning God: Grieving Loss, Wrestling with God, and Finding Your Way Back to Life

A NavPress resource published in alliance with Tyndale House Publishers

The Team:
David Zimmerman, Publisher; Caitlyn Carlson, Acquisitions Editor; Deborah Howell, Copyeditor; Lacie Phillips, Production Assistant; Ron C. Kaufmann, Cover Designer; Brandi Davis, Interior Designer; Sarah Ocenasek, Proofreading Coordinator

ISBN 978-1-64158-983-3

Printed in the United States of America

32 31 30 29 28 27 26
7 6 5 4 3 2 1

To David Allen Stein. Beloved son. February 20–April 14, 2018.

You and your little sister are my pride and joy, but it is you who made me a mommy and first taught me about the "Never Stopping, Never Giving Up, Unbreaking, Always and Forever Love"[1] *of God. Thank you for the honor of stewarding your story. I pray that I've told it well.*

To Mark Allen Stein. Beloved husband, father, and Papa. November 19, 1957–March 30, 2024.

For as long as I've known you, you asked when I was going to write a book. I never believed that I had anything to say, but you did. You had a way of seeing what people could become and lovingly drawing the best out of each of us. Thank you for believing in me and for sacrificially modeling the lavish love of the Father. Your generosity made this book possible.

To the women of Irving Bible Church, especially the women who journeyed alongside my family from 2017 to 2019.

Thank you for praying for me when I could not pray, for worshiping on my behalf when I had no songs to sing, and for bearing witness to my sorrow. You were the reason I got out of bed each morning after David died. Thank you for allowing me to pastor you through tears, for the abundant supply of hot tea and dark chocolate, and for continuing to speak my son's name. I love you.

Contents

INTRODUCTION

Losing God

The Christian life, from one angle, is the long journey of letting our natural assumption about who God is, over many decades, fall away, being slowly replaced with God's own insistence on who he is.

DANE ORTLUND, *GENTLE AND LOWLY*

All of us have multilayered portraits of who we think God is. As we've gone through life, we've shaped God according to our individual experiences. We've picked up stories about him along the way, imagined him to be like our parents (for better or worse), viewed him through our cultural ideology, and bumped into perceptions of him in hundreds of formative ways. In so doing, we've shaped a god who is small, known, comfortable, and manageable. Ours is a curated god.

But what happens to this curated image of God when your loved one dies or your spouse leaves you or you receive a terminal diagnosis? What happens when you lose your job or you slip back into addiction or the depression becomes treatment resistant? What then?

Most of us would like to think that we'd remain strong, faith intact and the hope of the gospel on our lips. But I've lived this raw *What then? What now?* And when I left the NICU for the final time, I lost both my infant son and the God I thought I knew. I'd expected to mourn David, but the sense of abandonment I felt by God blindsided me.

Don't worry: If you're already flinching and thinking that you don't have the emotional stamina to read about the loss of a child amid your own suffering and pain, this isn't a memoir. Our experience with David is a precious memory that the Lord has given to me, Jason, and a few family members and friends to cherish. But this is a book about you and me and God. It's a book for all of us who find that when the bottom falls out we aren't just grieving what we've lost—we're mourning the God we thought we knew.

THE PAIN OF EMOTIONAL DOUBT

When life as you knew it is falling apart, to sing "O death, where is your sting?" (1 Cor. 15:55, ESV) is like hurling a harpoon at your own heart and hoping you don't bleed.

"Christ Is Risen" is usually sung on Easter as a bold proclamation of the hope we have in Christ: "Come awake, come awake. Come and rise up from the grave."[1] But that assumes that you're worshiping on Easter, when new life abounds and graves are newly emptied. What do you sing when the grave is fresh? What do you declare when it's metaphorically, or literally, Good Friday and the sting of death is searing pain?

For six months, every time we sang that song at church, the only part I could resonate with was the anthem-like cry "Oh hell!"[2] To be a believer amid crisis is to have your faith tested and tried at every turn. You try to preach truth to yourself, but sometimes—many times—it falls flat. And the truest thing you may be able to declare is that you're walking through hell and don't have the strength to keep going.

Friend, there's no shame in acknowledging your life-upending grief. And there's no shame when that grief gets mixed with the dark clouds of doubt and morphs into grieving God himself. If you've ever found yourself disoriented, disappointed, frustrated, isolated, disillusioned, hopeless, and questioning everything about the God you thought you knew, you're in good company. You may even be walking on holy ground.

Dr. Barry Jones suggests that there are at least three kinds of doubt related to faith: intellectual, volitional, and emotional. Intellectual doubt asks, "Is it true?" and is born from the weight of uncertainty. Volitional doubt acknowledges, "I don't want it to be true" and results from the blindness created by pride. But the most common form of doubt, emotional doubt, emerges from the ache of pain and suffering and declares, "It doesn't feel true."[3]

There are apologetic and evangelistic tools, resources, and books ad nauseam to address the intellectual and volitional doubts someone may have about Christian belief, but what do we do with the complexities of emotional doubt?

My emotional doubt didn't come just from the pain of losing David. I also felt forsaken by God. I kept crying out, "God, where are you? *Where are you?*" I knew intellectually that if God was still with me he would provide the comfort and love necessary to sustain me through the loss of David. But if God wasn't present with me in my suffering—if he wasn't loving and good—then this journey wasn't worth walking. And frankly, life wasn't worth living.

Here's what I can tell you from years spent processing various traumatic losses while wrestling with God as well as over a decade of pastoral counseling experience: No matter the darkness, there is a hope that doesn't disappoint.

I don't know what darkness you find yourself in. I don't know what pain and heartache you bring to these pages. But I do know you are mourning the God you thought you knew. And I suspect you're yearning, hoping for something more. If you'll allow me, I'd like to be your companion on that journey.

Together we'll explore the invitation for you to move through mourning the God you thought you knew to intimately knowing the God who loves, comforts, walks with, and weeps with you. For it is in the painful stripping of false narratives about God—and the undoing that often results—that you have the opportunity to see God more clearly for who he is. That is the gift of this present season: to have your distorted views of God cast aside and replaced with a fuller understanding of the self-revealing God. *Ours is the God who comes near and mourns with us.*

PACKING FOR THE JOURNEY

Before we begin our journey, I'd like to suggest a few items to pack in your backpack. First, you'll want to carry our shared definition of *grief*:

> Grief is the loss of anything you weren't prepared to part with.

While I'm speaking from the perspective of losing my son (bereavement), our journey through this book is for mourning of *any* kind. I promise that there is something for me to learn in your story of mourning and for you to learn in mine.[4]

Second, you'll need a map of where we're headed and what you can expect along the way. As you've already experienced, the journey of grief is complex and disruptive. Grief comes out of experiencing the worst sort of change imaginable, and psychologists frequently describe acclimating to any sort of change as a three-step process: orientation, disorientation, and reorientation (although grief is not linear and you may experience this process multiple times). In many ways, this book follows that general approach, but it does so through the distinctive lens of the Christian story, tracing how the Man of Sorrows (Isa. 53:3, ESV)—Jesus himself—journeyed from death to resurrection life so that you and I and all creation might one day be set free from our groanings and experience true life *with him*.

We begin where you already are: in a graveyard confronting loss. In part 1, "Death," we'll explore the invitation to complain and cry out to God in the form of lament and reflect on the crucifixion of Christ, the ultimate act of love.

But sometimes the searing pain of grief can be so strong that it temporarily blinds you and casts you into darkness, which is the focus of part 2, "Darkness." As you grapple with an unseen opponent and the very real reality that God might not be who you thought he was, echoes of *Who and where are you, God?* bounce off the terrain. Together we'll examine the difficult yet sacred act of waiting in the dark for God to make himself known and the hope that can be birthed as you thirst for God's goodness.

Because God's silence is not his absence, darkness does eventually give way to light, and things become a bit clearer. Part 3, "Light," begins a season of reorientation where the nature of your grief and a greater awareness of the true God allow joy to comingle with your sorrow. In this new landscape, celebration becomes possible, as does increased trust in our risen God.

Finding your way back to the land of the living, we'll conclude the book with part 4, "Life." Jesus, the one who died for you, speaks to you, goes before you, and will one day dwell with you face-to-face, invites you to colabor with him in bringing beauty and redemption to our hurting world. In so doing, you get to actively participate in your own healing journey, help ease the pain of others, and declare that by God's power life triumphs over death.

Admittedly, when you and your faith are in survival mode, possibilities of new life may be the furthest thing from your mind—and that's okay. Allow me to do some of the heavy lifting for you and to point out places of potential healing as well as memorable vistas on our journey. I promise that there is still beauty, goodness, and truth to be found in your life.

Third, save the number of a licensed professional counselor in your phone. I'm serious. This book is not meant to be a replacement for counseling or therapy with a licensed practitioner. While spiritual counseling is of great value, its primary aim is to speak to your soul and to help you discern the will and ways of God in your life. However, professional counseling can specifically speak to your areas of hurt, such as grief, traumatic loss, abandonment, or rejection. I personally have benefited from counseling for over two decades, and I credit my licensed therapists for helping me be more mentally and emotionally healthy.

Finally, pack a water filter. By that I mean grant yourself permission to sift and filter through your beliefs, have faith-related doubt, ask hard questions, and refine your understanding of God. I'm not suggesting that you throw out an entire belief system. What I am suggesting is that you thoughtfully and intentionally engage in the process of examining—and if need be, dismantling—your faith so that the poisonous and untrue pieces can be discarded and you can reclaim and rebuild from that which is good and true. In other words, the journey we're on is a *refining* journey of spiritual growth, based on the self-revealing God who calls you and me to know him as he is revealed in his Word, through his Son, and through the indwelling of the Holy Spirit.

And I say *refining* because our faith won't be perfectly pure and without any degree of falsehood or sin until Jesus returns and our faith becomes sight. But that doesn't mean we don't endeavor to "lose our wrong ideas of God and the church" in the meantime.[5]

Now you stand at a crossroads, backpack packed. Will you keep your feet planted in despair and the fragments of your faith? Or will you take the first step into the swirling cloud of grief to see what, if anything, lies beyond? I hope you'll walk into the unknown with me, because the journey from disorientation to reorientation is an invitation to transformation (Rom. 5:3-5). You're invited to know God more fully and to learn to live and hope again.

PART 1

death

1

Death Can Go to Hell: *Grief*

"Death has been swallowed up in victory."
"Where, O death, is your victory?
Where, O death, is your sting?"

1 CORINTHIANS 15:54-55

Prior to David's death, I keenly felt the presence and goodness of God. In hundreds of ways, God kept reminding Jason and me that we weren't alone and that he was making a way for our family.

Nurses we didn't even know who attended our church were assigned to David's care and stayed long after their shifts to be present with us. Friends and family packed us up and moved us into a new apartment so that we came home to a stocked fridge and a decorated home complete with vases of fresh roses in February. Believers worldwide prayed for the healing of our son and sent hundreds of messages and cards of encouragement. And on day five of David's life, after we were told to say goodbye, he miraculously lived through the night and confounded doctors the next morning when they discovered that his heart was somehow stronger.

I had a mental image of Jason and me holding David and of Jesus wrapping his arms around all three of us in a strong and loving embrace. God was with us, and we would get through this, however it turned out.

But when David died, the image seemed to shift. It was as if Jesus was with us nearly to the end—until David exhaled his last breath, when Jesus released us from his embrace, got up, and walked out of the hospital room. I imagined Jesus standing outside in the hall, observing those precious final moments of David's life through the NICU window, just like the doctor and nurse who were respectfully distant but available should our family need them.

Then, once a few minutes had passed, I envisioned Jesus entering the room again and wrapping his arms around Jason and me, a family of three minus one. And I couldn't forgive God for walking out on us in our deepest moments of need, because in my opinion, friends don't abandon their loved ones in death.

DEATH SUCKS

So let's start there. There's likely been a catalytic event—your own version of death, whether literal or figurative—that has brought you to this point. Perhaps your child walked away from God, your spouse had an affair, or your best friend died unexpectedly. Maybe your pastor has been charged with abuse, your cancer is no longer in remission, or your company is cutting costs by laying you off. It's possible that your house has been foreclosed on, your adoption fell through, or mental illness is ravaging your family. You've lost something precious and have been ushered into a season of grief—grief of what was and of what could have been.

In your pain and desperation, you look for Jesus, the one who promised to never leave or forsake you, but now it seems he's nowhere to be found. Or perhaps, if you squint just right, you can make out an indistinct figure standing far off, watching you from a distance. Which is worse: for God to be completely absent or for him to be removed from and unmoved by your suffering? Either way, this is the sucker punch you didn't see coming, the secondary grief that comes from being stripped of the certainty you once had about God. It's a second death. And this is the one that cuts you, then guts you, and leaves you questioning everything. Because if you're now mourning God on top of grieving your original loss, who will carry you through this hell?

* * *

We all want a resurrection, but first there must be a death. And frankly, death sucks. It is the ultimate enemy of everything good, true, and beautiful in the world.

For millennia, people have struggled to reconcile God's love, goodness, and power with the presence of evil and suffering in the world. In fact, theodicy is an entire branch of philosophy devoted to addressing the problem of evil: If God is good, why does he allow evil to exist?[1]

Just as you and I can have similar and different stories, we each experience similar and different kinds of suffering, degrees of suffering, and causes of suffering. We cannot and should not paint suffering with one broad brushstroke.

In *Walking with God Through Pain and Suffering*, pastor and theologian Timothy Keller identifies four kinds of suffering in the Bible:[2]

1. *Suffering we bring on ourselves.* This type of suffering is directly caused by our own failures and is the consequence of sin. Jonah and David experienced this kind

of suffering. The invitation in this kind of suffering is to learn repentance.

2. *Suffering of betrayal.* This type of suffering is caused by bearing Jesus' name and may result in betrayal, persecution, or attacks from others. Jeremiah and Paul experienced this kind of suffering. The invitation in this kind of suffering is to practice love and extend forgiveness to your accuser.[3]

3. *Suffering of loss.* This type of suffering is caused by the grief of loss, be it the loss of finances, health, a relationship, a dream, trust, identity, circumstances, or a loved one. *This is the initial grief this book focuses on.* Mary and Martha experienced this kind of suffering when their brother, Lazarus, died. The invitation in this kind of suffering is to receive God's comfort and love and to fix your eyes on God.

4. *Suffering of mystery.* The cause of this type of suffering is ultimately unknown. It could result from the sins of another, the brokenness of the world, demonic powers, or something else. Job experienced this kind of senseless and mysterious suffering, which then led to him questioning God and the relationship he had once enjoyed with him. *The secondary grief we're exploring in this book—the loss of the God you thought you knew—is included in this category.* The invitation in this kind of suffering is to practice deliberate dependence on God.

In all four varieties of suffering, God invites the sufferer to grow spiritually and to become more like Jesus. And to be clear, this does not mean that the suffering itself is good. God can and does bring beauty from ashes and new life from death, but ashes and death are not good (Isa. 61:3; 1 Cor. 15:26). They are the evil results of living in a fallen, sin-soaked world in desperate need of redemption and restoration.

THE DEATH OF CERTAINTY

You and I were created for life and for uninterrupted, intimate relationships with God and others. Jesus said, "A thief is only there to steal and kill and destroy. I came so they can have real and eternal life, *more and better life* than they ever dreamed of" (John 10:10, MSG, emphasis mine). It sounds idyllic, doesn't it? So what happened to this spiritually flourishing and abundant life?

Well, thieves in the forms of sin, brokenness, and a pervasive desire to go our own way, do our own thing, and answer to no one entered the garden via the fall. And sin brought with it twin agonies:

(1) the pain of death and loss we're all well acquainted with and
(2) the breaking of relationship with God and the shattering of our certainty about who we believe God is and how we think God operates.

Let me explain. Yes, Adam and Eve ate the fruit after being instructed not to eat it. But the original sin wasn't one of coveting good food (although anyone who knows me knows that I don't like to go a day without hot tea, dark chocolate, and chips and salsa). Adam and Eve's sin was a lack of confidence in God and his goodness.

As finite creatures, Adam and Eve were limited. They didn't have unlimited power, unlimited presence, or unlimited knowledge like God did. And they were content with that for a time. Adam and Eve enjoyed a perfect relationship with each other and walked in the physical presence of God. They knew no shame and experienced the abundance of the world God had created for them to steward and cultivate as his image bearers.

And then the serpent, Satan, entered and sowed a seed of doubt: "Did God *really* say, 'You must not eat from any tree in the garden'?" (Gen. 3:1, emphasis mine). In other words, "Is God actually good? Does God *really* want good things for you? If so, why is he withholding this knowledge from you?" And when confronted with their limitations—with their physical inability to be God or at least manipulate and control God according to their desires—Adam and Eve rejected God's declaration over them as being "so very good" (Gen. 1:31, MSG).

As someone who has been plagued my entire life by a pervasive sense of shame and inadequacy at my core, I can't imagine the freedom and joy that comes from being created "so very good," even though, yes, I know that truth applies to me as well. I understand and resonate with Adam and Eve's desire for perfect knowledge of good and evil and with it the comfort that comes from certainty. And isn't that what we all want? Stability, safety, and security for us and our loved ones?

Yet Adam and Eve's literal grasping for control and certainty came at the cost of their confidence in God, the only one who truly is in control. As a result, Adam and Eve experienced the agony of death and loss (agony #1). A sacrificial animal was slaughtered to cover their nakedness (the first death in the history of the world).

Adam and Eve lost their home (exiled from Eden) and way of life. They stepped into a life of pain: painful toil in farming the land, pain in childbirth, and discord and misaligned desires in their marriage.

But even more painful was the shame and brokenness that now pervaded Adam and Eve's respective relationships with God and the undoing that resulted (agony #2). Adam and Eve likely had believed that life would *always* be as it was. They would *always* walk and talk with God in the garden of Eden. God would *always* provide for them. Their home would *always* be one of beauty and peace. Their children and the earth would *always* flourish. Adam and Eve had a certain view of God and expectations for how he would *always* act. But when the true God acted according to his will and not theirs, Adam and Eve found themselves undone, separated from God's physical presence, and literally uncovered.

Please hear me. I'm not suggesting that sin on your part is why God feels distant or you feel as if you no longer know who God is. But what we all share with Adam and Eve is this: Loss and the perception that God failed to act according to our expectations can all too easily propel us into disappointment and disillusionment with him.

Friend, what we need isn't illusory certainty. What we need is confidence—confidence in the person and promises of God, fueled by an intimate relationship with him. Living out of confidence in God is the only path through the pain and loss of our broken world.

But how can we move toward intimacy with and confidence in God when we feel like Jesus has left the room in our darkest hour and our faith seems to be fragmenting quickly? We must fight the urge to turn away and instead look at him unflinchingly with a question: *Who are you, God?*

TAKING GOD TO COUNSELING

Friends don't abandon their loved ones in death. If my refrain sounds familiar, it's because Mary and Martha echoed a similar cry when their brother, Lazarus, died (John 11:3, 21-22). We're going to explore Mary and Martha's story throughout this book, but for now, let's look at the setting.

> Now a man named Lazarus was sick. He was from Bethany, the village of Mary and her sister Martha. (This Mary, whose brother Lazarus now lay sick, was the same one who poured perfume on the Lord and wiped his feet with her hair.) So the sisters sent word to Jesus, "Lord, the one you love is sick."
>
> When he heard this, Jesus said, "This sickness will not end in death. No, it is for God's glory so that God's Son may be glorified through it." Now Jesus loved Martha and her sister and Lazarus. So when he heard that Lazarus was sick, he stayed where he was two more days, and then he said to his disciples, "Let us go back to Judea." (John 11:1-7)

First, notice the obvious: A man is sick and dying. Lazarus's illness is not attributed to personal sin, divine discipline, or a lack of God's love (see Eccles. 9:11; Luke 13:1-5; John 9:1-3). Lazarus is dying simply because he lives in a fallen world, where physical death reigns.

Second, notice that Jesus' love for Mary, Martha, and Lazarus is not in question. The sisters appeal to Jesus' professed love for Lazarus in verse 3, and the Gospel writer John affirms Jesus' love in verse 5. This family intimately knows Jesus, counts him as a close friend, has hosted him in their home, and number among his disciples. Yet Jesus intentionally chooses to delay traveling to see Lazarus, even though he knows Lazarus will die without his healing power.

And herein lies the tension. If Jesus is loving—and it's been established that he is—why does he allow Lazarus to die when he has the power to heal him?

Perhaps that's where you are today. You're not asking, *God, who are you?* in an intellectual or theoretical sense, because you know the truth of God's Word and have followed Jesus for a while. No, your questions in this season are experiential and come from the deepest recesses of your heart. They're personal questions about the very person and character of God, how he relates to you, and what he desires for you.

You're asking relationship questions. And if you didn't know it already: You're in relationship counseling with God.

Let me explain what I mean. I have lived with chronic depression and generalized anxiety for more than twenty years, and professional therapy continues to be one of the most beneficial tools in my mental-health journey. It's a safe and trusted place to wrestle with the difficult questions of life, share my disappointments, process my suffering, and receive insight and direction from my counselor. Honestly, I rarely enjoy the process of being in counseling (who delights in being utterly undone in front of someone else?), but I'm grateful for the hard work my counselor and I do together and for the fruit borne from taking intentional steps toward health and wholeness.

And so when I felt abandoned by God and couldn't see, feel,[4] or hear him in the wake of David's death, I did what seemed most natural: I took God to relationship counseling, metaphorically speaking.

God and I occupied this mental space for about six months. I imagined us to be in a small counseling room, sitting across from each other in two oversized chairs. This was relationship counseling, so of course we weren't sitting side by side on the couch. (That's only for couples in premarital counseling, who still daily text heart emojis to each other instead of important things like "Do we need milk?" and "Can you pick Katie up from school today?") There was never a counselor present, which I find odd in hindsight, but perhaps that's because my subconscious understood that I was in counseling with the Counselor himself. He was both the accused and the mediator.

After more than twenty-five years of walking intimately with God, I thought I knew who he was and how he operated. I thought we had a good relationship and enjoyed each other's company. But this betrayal—this abandoning Jason, David, and me to face death alone—was the breaking of a relationship. And there would be no coming back from it if God didn't start talking.

Mary and Martha cried to Jesus, "Lord, if you had been here, my brother would not have died" (John 11:21, 32), and my lament was similar. I cried, "God, if you were loving, you wouldn't have allowed David to die and then abandoned me in my grief."

So let's pause right there. You're in the metaphorical counseling room with God. Go ahead and mentally design a room where you feel as comfortable as possible. Rearrange the furniture to your liking, add plants and pillows, light a candle, install a few windows to let in natural sunlight, and add a therapy dog you can cuddle if that makes your heart sing. My counselor in real life, Sherry, has a goldendoodle named Cooper. That sweet dog allowed me to sob into his wavy fur for hours and never once shamed me for using an entire box of tissues in one session. (Thank you, Sherry and Cooper, for always keeping the Puffs lotion tissues stocked for me.)

And if needed, imagine a counselor or third party present. This can be a trusted person, an imaginary counselor of your liking, or even me if you so desire. This is your room, so try to imagine a space where you feel as safe and secure as possible.

Now, if you're able, state your question, complaint, or concern before God. It might be something like *God, if you were good, my friend wouldn't have been killed in a car accident.* Or *God, if you were merciful, my cancer wouldn't have come back.* Or perhaps *God, if you were my provider, I wouldn't have lost my job and had my house foreclosed on.*

Please be honest with yourself. In this season of disorientation, where everything seems to be sliding and shifting, you owe yourself the stability of truth. There's no shame in asking hard questions of God or investigating a belief you once held to be true. In fact, it takes great courage and vulnerability to evaluate your framework of beliefs and admit that you may need to refine some of them or even reject some altogether.

The good news is that if a belief is true it will hold up to scrutiny. And if it's not true, then that belief was never helping you anyway. In fact, it may have been harming you and holding you back from the fruitful life God desires for you and with you. So what question(s) do you have about God or for God?

SUFFERING AND THE HEART OF GOD

This side of heaven, you and I will likely never know the reason God has allowed such traumatic suffering and loss to come into our respective lives. And honestly, no intellectual reason would ever be worth the loss of my son. But in his great love, God did choose to explain why he allowed Lazarus to die.

> After he had said this, he went on to tell them, "Our friend Lazarus has fallen asleep; but I am going there to wake him up."
>
> His disciples replied, "Lord, if he sleeps, he will get better." Jesus had been speaking of his death, but his disciples thought he meant natural sleep.
>
> So then he told them plainly, "Lazarus is dead, and for your sake I am glad I was not there, so that you may believe. But let us go to him." (John 11:11-15)

Jesus allowed Lazarus to die so that when he later raised Lazarus from the dead (spoiler alert!), the disciples and onlookers would believe in Jesus (John 11:15, 42) and glorify God (John 11:4, 40). As Jesus said: "This sickness will not end in death. No, it is for God's glory so that God's Son may be glorified through it" (John 11:4).

This explanation may smart a little because you and I have received no such promise. Prior to Jesus' return, we aren't promised that what is dead and gone in our respective lives will once again rise to new life. You aren't given a promise that a new and better job will come along, that your estranged child will desire reconciliation, that the heart bypass surgery will be successful, or that your womb will be opened. What you are promised is the same promise that God gave to Israel: "I've never quit loving you and never will. Expect love, love, and more love!" (Jer. 31:3, MSG). Somehow love endures even when you feel like you can't.

For a month, my husband, Jason, and I literally sat in the dark praying and watching over our newborn son, cradled in his

Isolette, as his heart and lungs struggled to keep up with his growing body. Per protocol, nurses kept the shades drawn in David's NICU room, overhead lights were always off, and the only sounds to accompany our anxious thoughts were the alarms, beeps, and drips of the machines keeping David alive.

After the second failed attempt to take David off his ventilator, I realized my son would likely never be free of medical cords and that, short of God's divine intervention, he wasn't coming home from the hospital. Sitting in a rocking chair, half hidden by shadows, I was consumed by this new reality. I looked up at Jason across the sterile room and stated, "If David dies, I don't know if our marriage or my faith can survive." And without missing a beat, Jason turned from David toward me and replied, "Tiffany, my faith in God is strong, and my love for you is strong."

The agony of watching my son suffer and fearing his impending loss was so great that my hope had been crushed. But here was someone who loved me and truly knew me, who had promised to walk with me through it all. And in that moment I let Jason carry our hope because the weight of hope was too much for me to bear.

If you are despairing, if your confidence in God is shaken, if belief in his love and in his promises feels like a cruel trick, may I invite you to ask God who he is? To ask, *God, who are you?* and then sit in silence and sometimes darkness waiting for the great I Am to speak? This is the most important question you will ever ask. It's not something that requires misplaced hope, unearned trust, or suspended doubt. You may not yet be at a place where you have the desire or strength to look for God's love amid suffering, and that's okay. You've already taken the first step. You've shown up to relationship counseling with God, and that is enough.

REFLECTION QUESTIONS

1. Rate yourself on the scale below regarding your general desire for control.

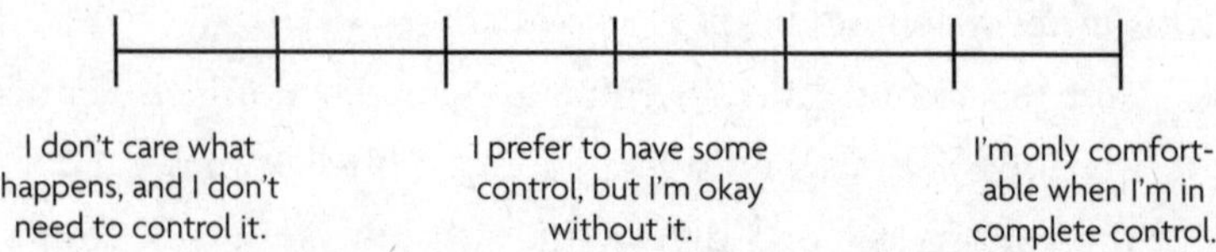

2. What do you think is the relationship between your desire for control and your current disappointment or disillusionment with God?

3. Imagine you're in the counseling room with God. State your question, complaint, or concern before him. Go ahead and write down any other questions you have about God or for God.

PRAYER

God, I'm hurting, I'm confused, and I don't know what to pray—and it doesn't always feel like prayer makes a difference. I long to know who you truly are, yet you remain a great mystery that I cannot fathom. In the spirit of Isaiah 40:28-29, I confess that I desire to know and hear from you. I need to receive strength from you, for I am weary and wrung out with grief. Please reveal yourself. Amen.

Do you not know?
  Have you not heard?
The Lord is the everlasting God,
  the Creator of the ends of the earth.
He will not grow tired or weary,
  and his understanding no one can fathom.
He gives strength to the weary
  and increases the power of the weak.

ISAIAH 40:28-29

2

Let It All Out: *Lament*

I'm standing my ground, God, shouting for help,
at my prayers every morning, on my knees each daybreak.
Why, God, do you turn a deaf ear?
Why do you make yourself scarce?

PSALM 88:13-14, MSG

I'm currently rearing an exuberant four-year-old with big emotions and big energy to match. I'm told that at preschool Emma Ruth is the teacher's helper and is obedient, respectful, quick to learn, and eager to assist (read *direct*) the other kids. Her teacher once leaned in and said to me, "She must be a joy at home." I smirked because, of course, Emma Ruth—along with her brother, David—is one of the greatest joys of my life. I love her fiercely, and she loves me back. Yet I'm on the receiving end of Emma Ruth's worst behavior. I'm the one she throws tantrums for, yells at, and pushes away.

After dwelling in parenting shame for weeks, I consulted my sister, who is a gifted marriage and family therapist with a specialty in early childhood. I confided, "I'm the one who spends the most time with Emma Ruth. I play with her, feed her, nurture her, and read to her, and together we go on lots of fun adventures. I cuddle her, sing to her, and set firm and loving boundaries. I'm not a pushover. What am I doing wrong?" My sister answered, "Research has shown that children display the worst behavior with those they are most comfortable with. Because she has a safe and secure attachment to you, she feels that she can be herself around you."

Ah! Because I'm not going anywhere, because I love her unconditionally, because she knows I will meet her needs *no matter what*, Emma Ruth lets her guard down with me and expresses her full range of emotions. And in a way that only a preschooler can, she shows that she loves me—by letting it all out.

THE LANGUAGE OF SUFFERING

Children may feel safe and secure enough to let out all their emotions with the people who love them most, but many of us struggle to do that as adults. In the throes of grief, we'll do almost anything to avoid the pain and suffering that accompany loss. Some of us throw ourselves into work or zealous exercise. Others of us eat the entire pan of dark chocolate brownies or binge-watch all seven seasons of our favorite show on Netflix. Still others cram their schedules with endless activities, while some lie in bed mindlessly scrolling through Instagram and refusing to answer the phone when friends call to check in. Be it numbing, self-medicating, avoiding, distancing, and/or disconnecting, we all have coping strategies. The question isn't whether you have a coping strategy, because you do. The question is: Is it a helpful strategy?

The pain is something you must work through to move forward. You can't go over, under, or around it. The only way to get unstuck—to keep growing—is to let it all out and move through the pain. For those of us wrestling with God in our grief, Scripture gives us a way to do that: lament.

Lament is challenging for us for the same reason we often turn to unhealthy coping strategies in our pain: In our Western culture, we don't know how to face grief well. As Soong-Chan Rah writes in *Prophetic Lament*, "the American church avoids lament. . . . The absence of lament in the liturgy of the American church results in the loss of memory. We forget the necessity of lamenting over suffering and pain. We forget the reality of suffering and pain."[1]

Lament is a churchy word that has to do with crying out to God in times of distress or despair. It is the language of suffering. If you're living in the disorientation phase of grief, you've probably been lamenting, even if you didn't know it's called that. *I wish I wasn't here! This shouldn't be happening! God, help me! Rescue me! Make all the pain go away!* To lament is simply to turn toward God in prayer with your complaints and concerns as opposed to turning away from him. It's a way to authentically process your grief with God—even if it's about him.

Of course, in the very real mental, emotional, and physical pain of grief, a few objections to this kind of raw honesty might come to mind:

- *Lament seems painful. Why should I practice it?*
- *I'm uncertain about or doubting God. Why would I process with him?*
- *I don't want to anger or disrespect God with my true feelings. Can I really be honest with him?*

Why Lament?

The good news is that you've already taken your first steps on the journey of lament. You've acknowledged your loss. You're reading this book and naming your concerns, questions, and doubts before God. Those are all steps of courageous engagement, and taking them is something to be proud of. Because the truth is that not everyone is willing to do the hard work of pushing through the pain in pursuit of hope and healing.

That leads us to the bad news: It may get worse before it gets better. To process and wrestle through the pain, you must stop running from the pain and sit with it, explore it, and feel the weight of it. Patrick O'Malley, primary author of *Getting Grief Right* and a respected psychotherapist, writes, "The goal is to stay present to your grief story, as painful as it might be, and to try not to run from it. However you might try to escape, grief will be waiting for you, in one form or another."[2]

To mourn is to choose to actively engage with your grief or sorrow. No one else can do it for you. Much like you wouldn't just watch your personal trainer do bicep curls and expect *your* body to become more physically fit (I wish!), *you* have to show up, sweat, and push through the resistance (pain) as you strive for greater health. Pursuing healing is a hard-won gift you give yourself day in and day out as you choose to engage with the process of grieving.

And let's be honest: The healing journey takes time—so very much time (we'll talk more about that in part 2). In a society of instant everything, we want the pain gone instantly, or at least after whatever period we think is appropriate for mourning. But friend, life isn't like that. Healing from loss is a journey, and like Jacob, who wrestled with God (Gen. 32:22-32), we may always walk with a limp thereafter.

So why lament? Because it's a necessary part of the healing process. Why engage with the pain of your grief? Because it's the only way forward to a life of thriving and not just surviving.[3]

Why Lament to God?

You may be asking, *If I'm uncertain about God or doubting God, why would I process with him?* Because you already have a relationship with him.

Hear me out. Doubting or questioning God usually only happens because you had a relationship with him to begin with. You thought you knew God, and now it feels like he has let you down and you're confused about who he truly is. But when someone you love lets you down, you don't just cut them off. Instead, you tell them how hurt you are and invite them into a conversation in hopes of working through it together. After all, you wouldn't be reading this book if some small part of you didn't believe (or want to believe) it is worth wrestling with God about your tender places of hurt.

Remember, lament is a form of petition for change from someone you believe is powerful and cares. It's an expression of trust and, in some cases, desperation. And it's okay if you're more in the desperate state than in the trusting state. That's literally why lament exists—so you can wail and cry out about the broken things of life to someone who truly cares and has the power to change them. Thankfully, your degree of confidence about who God is doesn't change the certainty of who he is.

Can I Really Be Honest Before God?

The third objection is one that often arises when we start talking about lament: *Can I really be honest before God? Can I bring my true thoughts and feelings before him without fear he'll be angry with me or punish me for being disrespectful?*

Yes, you can complain to God about God. Does that blow your mind? I've tried doing that with other people, but for some reason, complaining about my husband to my husband never gets the results I'm hoping for. And yet, God, your ever-loving Father, invites you to bring everything—including your grievances, grumblings, and accusations—to him.

Why? Because God loves you. Because he longs to be in an intimate relationship with you. Because he already knows your thoughts and feelings anyway and isn't threatened by you questioning him. And because you have Jesus, your High Priest, who is able to "sympathize with our weaknesses" (Heb. 4:15, ESV).

Dane Ortlund, author of *Gentle and Lowly*, writes:

> [The word for] "sympathize" here is not cool and detached pity. It is a depth of felt solidarity such as is echoed in our own lives most closely only as parents to children. Indeed, it is deeper even than that. In our pain, Jesus is pained; in our suffering, he feels the suffering as his own even though it isn't—not that his invincible divinity is threatened, but in the sense that his heart is feelingly drawn into our distress. His human nature engages our troubles comprehensively. *His is a love that cannot be held back when he sees his people in pain.*[4]

One of the beautiful truths about the Christian faith is that we are invited to come as we are before God. You don't have to clean up your life, say the right words, do the correct things, get yourself together, or become a "good" person to address God. You've already been granted access to God, thanks to the saving work of Jesus on the cross. The author of Hebrews continues, "Let us then approach God's throne of grace with confidence, so that we may receive mercy and find grace to help us in our time of need" (Heb. 4:16).

Don't miss this: Because Jesus knows what it is to suffer, in his perfect love he draws near to you in times of distress. *And* he invites you to approach the throne of the Father with the confidence of someone who knows that they will be lavishly given mercy and grace in seasons of suffering. Jesus draws near. The Father provides.

BIBLICAL LAMENT: A HOLY OCCUPATION

It's in this context of relational love and provision that we're invited to lament. In the Bible, countless individuals practice lament. And by nature of it being lament, it wasn't pretty. Their lament is raw, real, and messy.

Job cursed the day he was born because of his overwhelming suffering (Job 3:1). The enslaved Israelites cried out to God for deliverance from their Egyptian oppressors (Exod. 2:23) and then, once delivered, complained, "It would have been better for us to serve the Egyptians than to die in the desert!" (Exod. 14:12). Naomi asked her neighbors to call her Mara, which means "bitter," because "the Almighty has made my life very bitter" (Ruth 1:20). King David penned, "My God, my God, why have you forsaken me? Why are you so far from saving me, so far from my cries of anguish?" (Ps. 22:1). Each of these people bravely chose to talk to God about their pain instead of simply being a reservoir of pain.

The place we learn the most about what lament looks like in the life of a believer is in Psalms, Israel's hymnbook. In a book of songs and prayers sung both individually and corporately, it might seem odd to include psalms of lament along with psalms of thanksgiving, praise, petition, and confession. Yet their inclusion shows us that lament isn't merely normal in the Christian life; it is a holy occupation.

Psalms 42 and 43

Psalms of lament, like Psalms 42 and 43,[5] typically contain four basic elements: *turn*, *complain*, *ask*, and *trust*.[6] As we've previously discussed, the first step of lament is a turn toward God. The author of Psalm 42 writes, "As the deer pants for streams of water, so my soul pants for you, my God" (Ps. 42:1). This ongoing prayer dialogue with God gives you a safe place to process the good, bad, and ugly of all that is going on with someone who truly loves and cares for you.

Having turned toward God, the next step is complaint, probably the easiest and most natural element of the lament process. Pastor Mark Vroegop, author of *Weep with Me: How Lament Opens a Door for Racial Reconciliation*, states, "Biblical complaint vocalizes circumstances that do not seem to fit with God's character or his purposes."[7] In lamenting, you have an opportunity to express to God the very real tension between what you're experiencing and what you know to be true of him. Notice the tension in Psalm 42:9, as paraphrased in *The Message*: "Sometimes I ask God, my rock-solid God, 'Why did you let me down? Why am I walking around in tears, harassed by enemies?'"

After you have expressed the lived tension and resulting suffering, complaint gives way to making an ask of God in alignment with his character and promises. The psalmist pleads, "Vindicate me. . . . Rescue me. . . . Send me your light and your faithful care, let them lead me; let them bring me to your holy mountain, to the place where you dwell" (Ps. 43:1, 3). When you pray according to God's will, you are in essence asking for God's reign to be realized on the earth as it is in heaven. You're asking for relief from pain, for deliverance from suffering, for the elimination of evil, and for flourishing and new life to take place. As one of my favorite Bible teachers and mentors, Alice McQuitty, likes to say, "These are prayers that God always answers."[8]

Vroegop makes the point that we often feel we must believe *before* we can ask. Thankfully, however, it is often our asking that leads to the deepening of our beliefs. For in the asking we're reminded of what we believe and where our hope and trust are placed. As Timothy Keller summarizes in *Walking with God Through Pain and Suffering*, "this is not forcing yourself to feel in a certain way but rather directing your thoughts until your heart, sooner or later, is engaged."[9]

The desired conclusion of turning, complaining, and asking is renewed trust in God. Vroegop explains, "Laments help us through suffering by directing our hearts to make the choice—often daily—to trust in God's purposes hidden behind the pain. In this way, a lament is one of the most theologically informed practices of the Christian life."[10] Having rehearsed to himself God's faithfulness in his own life, the psalmist concludes by exhorting his soul, "Put your hope in God, for I will yet praise him, my Savior and my God" (Ps. 43:5).

Notice the *yet*. It's future oriented, as in "Hope in God; for I *shall again* praise him" (Ps. 43:5, ESV, emphasis mine). In so doing, the psalmist is reaching into the future and declaring that its implications are true right now, *today*. It's as if he's saying, "Because God has been faithful in the past [remembering], and because he will be faithful in the future [hoping], I can trust him right now."

Note that this four-part structure of the psalms of lament is generalized. It's not meant to be formulaic or to feel forced. It's meant as a scaffold on which to hang your own complaints and requests of God. And if trying to get to the desired conclusion of greater trust in God seems like leaping off your scaffolding and free-falling ten stories, take heart. There is a psalm for you.

Psalm 88

Of the roughly sixty-five psalms of lament, Psalm 88 is the only one that doesn't get resolved. The author, Heman the Ezrahite, was "one of the singers in King David's procession when the ark of the covenant was brought to Jerusalem," and he is described later as "'the king's seer' and music director for the temple"[11] (see 1 Chron. 6:33-38; 15:17-19; 25:4-6).

In other words, Heman played an important role in both composing and leading Tabernacle worship for all Israel, and yet, in this psalm, Heman doesn't praise God or end with hope in him. In fact, Heman directly blames God for his calamities, saying, "You have put me in the lowest pit" and "Your wrath lies heavily on me" (Ps. 88:6-7). He accuses God of rejecting him and hiding his face from him (Ps. 88:14) and then concludes, "You have taken from me friend and neighbor—darkness is my closest friend" (Ps. 88:18). In this psalm, Heman literally believes that darkness will have the last word in his life.*

While Psalm 88 is never going to be part of a sermon series on joy, if you're having a terrible, no good, very bad season, there is a unique comfort and solace in finding out that you're not alone. Others have felt this way too, professional worship leaders included.

Your experience of not having anything good to say to God in

* If you're contemplating suicide or thinking that others would be better off without you, please tell a trusted friend or family member *and* reach out to a professional therapist or doctor. If you need immediate help, call 988 or visit 988lifeline.org for 24/7 free and confidential support.

the moment is valid, and God invites and receives your lament, even when you can't wrap it up in a shiny bow of trust.[12]

One scholar writes about Psalm 88, "The psalmist can barely grasp a few hints about his positive feelings toward God. For example, he affirms his relationship with God, calling him 'the God who saves me' (v. 1), and he prays to this God (vv. 2, 9, 13); he also assumes that praise is the normal mode of life, and he wants to return to that mode (vv. 10-12). But his feelings are overwhelmingly negative. The psalm thus exemplifies a believer's proper response in the depths of despair, when sometimes all one can do is pour out one's heart to God and simply wait."[13]

The mind-boggling fact is that God felt that Heman's raw, unfiltered expression of the human experience was important enough to be included in the Bible. In this psalm, there is no pretense, no appearance of pleasantness, no fear of repercussions for addressing God like this, and certainly no nuancing or sidestepping of the uncomfortable emotions the author feels. Instead, Heman prays from the depths of his soul. And you and I are invited to do so as well, whether our lament looks like Psalm 88 or Psalms 42 and 43.

WHAT ABOUT TODAY?

So how do you engage with the practice of lament while waiting for resolution?

Pray God's Word

When you're weary, your soul feels dry, you lack faith, or you have no words at all, you can pray the Word of God back to God. The lament psalms encompass everything from grief to suffering and from cries for deliverance from enemies to cries for justice for the oppressed. If there is hurt, loss, or pain, there is a lament psalm for it. The value in praying through the lament psalms includes immersing yourself in Scripture, continuing to dialogue with the God who listens and cares, and situating yourself within a biblical and historical tradition.†

In addition to the lament psalms, you can read and pray through the books of Job and Lamentations. The book of Job is about a man who lived during the time of the patriarchs. Job was a righteous man whom God allowed Satan to attack and test, although Job didn't know that that's what was happening. He suffered the loss of his children, livestock, home, servants, and physical health, a series of events that would fall into Keller's category of suffering of mystery (see chapter 1).

Throughout the book, Job calls on God to deliver him from his unjust suffering and to explain why he is experiencing such catastrophic loss. Job's self-righteous friends attempt to determine the cause of his suffering and only make matters worse with their moralistic solutions. At the end of the book, God responds to Job, but he doesn't explain the reason for Job's suffering. Instead, he reminds Job of his power, wisdom, and loving-kindness as well as his omnipotence and his deep care and concern for the world from the very first day of creation. God rebukes Job's friends and blesses Job.

Pay attention to what questions Job asks of God and to the suppositions he and his friends make about God. You might want to make some of their laments to God your own. However, some of their prayers reflect their distorted image of God. When you come across a distortion, allow it to prompt you to pray and ask God to bring you greater understanding of who he is in your lamenting.

---

† For a list of suggested psalms to begin with, visit tiffanystein.com.

The book of Lamentations consists of five poems that mourn the destruction of Jerusalem in 586 BCE by the Babylonians.[14] "In Lamentations, the poet grieves, yet still has faith—crying out to God for mercy."[15] An example of communal lament, Lamentations falls into the category of suffering we bring on ourselves, since God allowed the Israelites to be exiled due to their repeated turning away from him, disobedience, idolatry, and refusal to repent. "These laments should be regarded not as simply an emotional outpouring but as a deliberate attempt to explore the possibility that the relationship between God and people can be restored."[16]

As you read, identify the four basic elements of lament in Lamentations and what specifically leads to the author expressing renewed trust and hope in God. (Hint: Look at Lamentations 3:19-26). Pray Lamentations 3:19-26 back to God and ask that he will grant you the desire and ability to remember his goodness.

Write Your Own Lament

Writing your own prayer of lament can be both clarifying and healing as you let everything out on paper. Not only does a written lament help you process through your sorrow with the great Healer, but it can serve as a signpost later in your faith story. One day you might be able to look back on your lament and see God's hand of faithfulness, even though where you are seems dark right now.

If you need a structure to follow, try Vroegop's model of *turn*, *complain*, *ask*, and *trust*.

Turn: Address God.

Complain: What grieves or pains you? What is going on that seems inconsistent with God's character, promises, and plans as you understand them?

Ask: What would you like to see God do that is in alignment with who he is? Be specific. Pray boldly and with courageous conviction.

Trust: If you're able, express your trust or confidence in God. Praise him for who he is and what he has done in your life.

Pray God's Promises

When the uncertainty of life is overwhelming and you're in desperate need of a stable place on your journey to rest a bit, pray toward believing God's promises. I'm not suggesting you should take verses out of context and name and claim things like perfect health, financial wealth, or career success. Instead, pray promises tied to God's character and will. In other words, pray that you'll have greater belief and confidence in who God says he is and what he says he'll do.

What promises can you grab hold of? What verses can ground you and bring you back to center when things seem unsteady? Ask the Holy Spirit for wisdom and discernment as you search the Scriptures.‡

Lament in Community

When we practice lament in community, we tangibly "rejoice with those who rejoice; mourn with those who mourn" (Rom. 12:15). One of the gifts of being part of the body of Christ is that you belong to a worldwide body of sisters and brothers who bear both your joys and your sorrows. We were created to do life together, and just as you wouldn't live in isolation apart from the love of others, you wouldn't want to lament in isolation either.

If you're unfamiliar with corporate lament, that's okay. It's a new practice for some. To lament with others is to share solidarity with and participate in their pain and suffering. It requires vulnerability, courage, and humility to invite others into your pain. And it requires wisdom, compassion, and empathy to enter into the pain of others.

In the individualistic West, where requesting help or admitting pain is often perceived as inadequacy and weakness, sharing your burden with others may seem like a terrible idea. Particularly if your pain is tied to the sin of you or loved ones, you risk judgment and rejection. However, if the person or people you're inviting into your story truly exhibit the love and grace of God, they'll receive your story with respect and discernment, holding it safely while walking alongside you in your healing journey.

Practically speaking, corporate lament can take many forms.

‡ For a list of promises you may want to consider, visit tiffanystein.com.

It can look like your church hosting regular times of corporate lament during which the sins of the community are confessed and together you call out to God for justice and racial reconciliation. It might look like you asking the people in your small group to lament with you via prayer the trauma and abuse you experienced as a child and join you in prayer for God to bring healing. It could look like you calling a friend and sharing your confusion regarding God's silence in the midst of heartache and her mailing you a card that simply says, "I see you and your pain. I'm sorry. I lament with you and will continue praying."

If you don't have a safe and trusted person with whom you can share your pain, please look for a Christian support group or licensed Christian counselor in your area. If you need references or recommendations, local churches should be able to provide you with a list of resources in your region.

And when you get to a season where life is a little less painful and you have the emotional bandwidth to do so, give the gift of lament to someone else. Lamenting with and accompanying those who are hurting is a form of sacrificial love that bears fruit for both the giver and the receiver. You don't have to do it perfectly (you can't) or have the right words to say (you won't) or know how to fix it for them (you can't). You simply show up, bear witness to their pain, and say, "I am with you." To have a friend draw near in the darkness—is there a greater gift?

A LIMITED PERSPECTIVE

As you learn the language of lament and further lean into its rhythms, remember this: Lament expresses the truth of what you're feeling in that moment (or season), not necessarily the truth of who God is. Scholar John Barry remarks, "Despite being accusatory of Yahweh, [lament psalms] actually express faith in Him by directing concerns to Him. The accusations of Yahweh do not necessarily accurately depict Yahweh's character or His actual role in the psalmist's life—instead, they express the emotion of the psalmist toward Yahweh."[17]

In other words, perspective is essential to practicing biblical lament. Each lament psalm is written by a specific author in a specific time and place for a specific reason. No one psalm contains a lifetime of prayer. Instead, each psalm is a snippet of the author's complete faith story and dialogue with God.

Thus, by nature of it being time bound, lament's perspective is always limited. In the depths of despair, Heman shows us in Psalm 88 that pain isn't always neatly resolved in a single prayer. *Resolution has not yet occurred.* On the other hand, Psalm 42 shows us the author's ability to look back and see God's hand of goodness at work, which gives him hope in present circumstances. *Resolution is in the process of occurring.*

And one day *true and final resolution will occur.* The beautiful reality is that we won't need the psalms of lament once Jesus returns. Lament is a useful tool only as long as sin and death exist. So in the meantime, continue to complain and cry out to God. His shoulders are wide enough to take it all—and still hold you.

REFLECTION QUESTIONS

1. What are your current coping strategies for the grief you're experiencing? Are these coping mechanisms truly helping you heal?

2. Which objection(s) to lament most resonate(s) with you and why?

3. Which practice of lament will you try today?

4. How does the practice of lament help you better understand God as he really is and not as you wish him to be?

PRAYER

God, I'm learning that it's okay, even good, to lament to you. And so I confess [grief, pain, apparent inconsistencies in God's character and actions, etc.]. Would you meet me in this place of deep sorrow and doubt? You know I long for resolution, not just when you return but now. Help me trust you in the waiting. Amen.

Because of the Lord's great love we are not consumed,
for his compassions never fail.

LAMENTATIONS 3:22

3

The One Who Died for You: *Love*

About three in the afternoon Jesus cried out in a loud voice,
"Eli, Eli, lema sabachthani?" *(which means "My God, my God,*
why have you forsaken me?").

MATTHEW 27:46

For he has not despised or scorned
the suffering of the afflicted one;
he has not hidden his face from him
but has listened to his cry for help.

PSALM 22:24

It's hard to find something worth living for when what or whom you'd die for is already gone.[§]

But I was being watched. It was one of the main reasons I even bothered to get out of bed each morning after David died.

Our grief was a public one. Both Jason and I were pastors of Irving Bible Church, a megachurch in Dallas, Texas, and thousands had journeyed with us through my pregnancy, David's life

§ If you are struggling to see purpose or meaning in your life, please reach out to a professional therapist as well as a trusted family member or friend. If you need immediate help, call 988 or visit 988lifeline.org for 24/7 free and confidential support.

and death, and now the aftermath. I was keenly aware that I had an audience of people who depended on me and needed me to authentically show up—tears, dark circles under my eyes, unanswered questions, and all. Because not only was I hurting, grieving, and confused about God, but so were the four hundred or so women I knew intimately and pastored in women's Bible study.

These precious women had expectantly hoped and prayed for the healing of David's heart. They had gathered their friends, neighbors, coworkers, and prayer partners around the world to intercede on our behalf. They had fasted, lamented, held twenty-four-hour prayer vigils, canceled Bible study for a day of intercessory prayer and worship, and done all the "right" things. Death of a beloved baby was not what they had expected of a good God. My dear friend and coworker Amy summarized the group's sentiment perfectly: "God, you got this one wrong."

As their shepherd, I hurt with and for them. I didn't want to walk through this suffering, and I didn't want them to have to walk through it either.

And so I knew it was time. Time to see if what I preached on stage about the goodness and love of God was also true in the cemetery. They were watching me, and honestly, I was watching myself too.[1]

PUNCTUATED POSTURE

When God behaves in a way you didn't expect, when circumstances appear contrary to his will, and when, after doomscrolling through your news feed, the world generally seems to be falling apart, the most natural response is accusation: *God, who are you!*

There's a world of difference between that and *God, who are you?*, and I'm not just talking about the punctuation.

The difference lies in your posture. The accusatory exclamation point says, *Prove yourself, God! You said you're good, kind, loving, and just. Now* show *me. Defend your actions!* It's the posture that declares that there are two sides: Someone will be right, and someone will be wrong. And who wants to be wrong?

But if you ask, *God, who are you?*, you intentionally approach him with a posture of curiosity and receptivity. Your question then becomes an invitation to dialogue: *Help me understand, God. I thought you were good, kind, loving, and just, but the circumstances make it seem otherwise. What happened here? Am I missing something?* You're no longer in a zero-sum game but rather participating in a conversation in which you seek to know and be known in hopes of deepening the relationship.

At the time of David's death, I believed that if God was good and loving, as his Word says he is, he wouldn't have allowed David to die and then abandoned me in my grief. I mistakenly framed God's love as an either-or proposition (which is dangerous, because either-or thinking oversimplifies the situation and neglects the possibility of additional options), and that left me with only two possible options:

1. God is not loving, the loss of David is senseless and cruel, and this is not a god I want to know (posture of attack and accusation).
2. God is loving, and in some mysterious way I can't comprehend, God's love is big enough to include the loss of David (posture of curious receptivity).

I initially vacillated between the two postures, but once I began leaning into lament—realizing that my anger at God was masking my deep hurt at feeling abandoned by him and that God was okay with my anger—I became more willing to dialogue with him. I still didn't have any answers, but I was willing to explore the possibility that there might be more than my limited perspective allowed.

You see, the second posture requires suspended judgment. It requires choosing to believe that there will always be a gap between the fullness of the triune God and our limited understanding of him. And therein lies the challenge. You and I are invited to know God as he is—as revealed in his Word, through his Son, and through the indwelling of the Holy Spirit—not as we would wish, imagine, or expect him to be.[2]

So who is he?

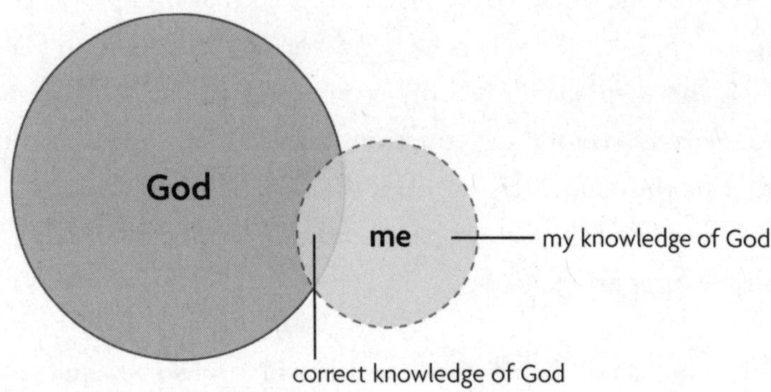

GOD'S LOVE REVEALED IN EXODUS 34

Think back on some of your first memories of God. How were you introduced to him? Who or what were the main sources that contributed to your understanding of God?

My first memories of God are intertwined with fear. I was a toddler, and while my parents were extremely loving, the church I grew up in was not. It focused on moralistic performance, on not forfeiting one's salvation due to disobedience, and on being set apart from the "corrupting" influences of the world. To me, God was an invisible spiritual being with a grim frown who was constantly displeased with me and eager to punish me or my family if we sinned too greatly. Fear of God was the shadow always with me, and I had frequent nightmares about judgment day. Because I knew how disobedient my heart was, I believed God could never love me.

And yet this is not how Scripture depicts God. This is not who God says he is!

After delivering the Israelites from slavery in Egypt, Moses was struggling to lead the stiff-necked Israelites, who preferred the certain death of slavery in Egypt to the unforeseeable future of journeying through the wilderness, to the Promised Land. God promised to go with them and give them rest (Exod. 33:14), but it wasn't enough for Moses. Perhaps still fearful of God abandoning them in their waywardness, Moses asked God to reassure him about who he really was: "Please, let me see your glory" (Exod. 33:18, CSB).

Instead of rebuking Moses for his question regarding his identity or belittling his small faith, God replied, "I will cause all my goodness to pass in front of you, and I will proclaim my name, the LORD, in your presence" (Exod. 33:19). Dane Ortlund says of what happened next, "Short of the incarnation itself, this is perhaps the high point of divine revelation in all the Bible"[3]: "He passed in front of Moses, proclaiming, 'The LORD, the LORD, the compassionate and gracious God, slow to anger, abounding in love and faithfulness, maintaining love to thousands, and forgiving wickedness, rebellion and sin. Yet he does not leave the guilty unpunished; he punishes the children and their children for the sin of the parents to the third and fourth generation'" (Exod. 34:6-7).

Ortlund summarizes this theophany, an appearance of God,

this way: "When God himself sets the terms on what his glory is, he surprises us into wonder. Our deepest instincts expect him to be thundering, gavel swinging, judgment relishing. We expect the bent of God's heart to be retribution to our waywardness. And then Exodus 34 taps us on the shoulder and stops us in our tracks. *The bent of God's heart is mercy. His glory is his goodness.*"[4]

Our God—the God you and I worship—is overflowing with abundant mercy and grace. "Everything the Lord says autobiographically is something that God is or does for the benefit of others, especially his chosen people."[5] God's natural inclination, his default mode, is compassion and grace.[6] And from that abundant mercy and grace stream love, faithfulness, and forgiveness.

You and I are primed for anger. How easily do you go from calm to irate over someone cutting you off in traffic? If your spouse loads the dishwasher incorrectly, do you immediately become disgruntled? What happens when you've waited ten minutes in line for your coffee and the person in front of you *still* can't decide what to order? Anger, irritability, resentment, aggravation, and bitterness come naturally and swiftly for us. But not for God. God is slow to anger. He must be provoked to anger, because he is love (1 John 4:16).

And don't let Exodus 34:7 trip you up. Yes, God is just and good, and therefore he will punish those who continue to walk in the sins of their parents. But what lasts longer, God's love or God's discipline? God's love! The discipline and correction of God last for a short time (and honestly, discipline *is* part of love), while his love lasts for thousands of generations.[7] *God's love has the final say.*

This isn't just a onetime occurrence in the Bible. God is consistent in letting us know who he is. The Bible weaves a seamless narrative of God's "Never Stopping, Never Giving Up, Unbreaking, Always and Forever Love" from Genesis to Revelation.[8]

If this understanding of God is new to you, pause and sit with the truth until it begins to sink in. If it's something you already believe but not something that feels true in the moment, pray and ask the Holy Spirit to move you from intellectual assent to heart conviction. Pray:

> *God, you have revealed yourself to be the God of compassion, love, forgiveness, and faithfulness. I want to believe, but my current circumstances seem contrary to your character. Please help my unbelief (Mark 9:24). Please help me see and understand you as you truly are. Grow my trust in you. Amen.*

It's worth meditating and reflecting on who God reveals himself to be—compassionate, gracious, slow to anger, just, forgiving, and abounding in love and faithfulness—because it's through this lens that we're to read the Bible and understand our circumstances.

WHAT ABOUT MY PAIN?

After David's death, I still believed what I had preached so many times about the God of love and grace, who is near to the suffering. But I'll be honest: The lens of Exodus 34 wasn't enough for my grieving heart. It isn't very comforting to just know that God cares for you. You want to know that God is going to *do something* about your pain.

Around 740 BCE, Isaiah prophesied about the Suffering Servant, whom we now know to be Jesus:

> Surely he took up our *pain*
>   and bore our *suffering*,
> yet we considered him *punished* by God,

stricken by him, and *afflicted.*
But he was *pierced* for our transgressions,
he was *crushed* for our iniquities;
the *punishment* that brought us peace was on him,
and by his *wounds* we are healed.
We all, like sheep, have gone astray,
each of us has turned to our own way;
and the LORD has laid on him
the iniquity of us all. . . .
For he *bore the sin of many,*
and made intercession for the transgressors.
(Isa. 53:4-6, 12, emphasis mine)

Notice the language used to describe what Jesus was going to experience. He was going to experience "pain," "suffering," and "punishment" at the hand of the Father as he "bore the sin of many." Jesus was going to be "stricken," "afflicted," "pierced," "crushed," and literally bear "wounds" for our healing. To do something about our pain (not just the pain of our grief but the pain of being dead in our sins and separated from the living God), God himself was going to not only experience his own pain but also take on my pain, your pain, and that of the entire world. And that he did.

Roughly 770 years later, Isaiah's prophecy was fulfilled when God conclusively did something about humanity's pain and proved, once and for all, who he is and what he is about: Jesus went to the cross.

But we're a forgetful people. I know I am. And that is one of the reasons why the universal church traditionally rehearses and remembers the events from the last week of Jesus' life during Holy

Week, the last week of Lent.[¶] Just as Jesus identifies with our suffering, we're invited to identify with Jesus' forty days in the wilderness and his dying (Rom. 6:5; 2 Cor. 4:10-11), collectively calling out, *God, do something about the pain!*

Almost a year after David's death, I wrote in my journal,

> A year ago this evening, I was imposing ashes on [members of my church]. It was Ash Wednesday; we were entering into Lent, and it was a somber and reflective time. We knew about David's heart condition, and I was going in for weekly sonogram appointments, hoping to carry him as long as possible so that he didn't have additional complications resulting from coming early and his lungs not being fully developed.
>
> I was sad and tense, and fear was the undercurrent of my every day. And on this night a year ago, David and I—me pregnant and full of life and all its potential—imposed ashes. It was my first time to participate in this ritual, and I was honored. I mixed water with the ashes of last year's palm fronds [from Palm Sunday, when the church traditionally remembers the entrance of Jesus into Jerusalem by waving palm fronds] and recited over my brothers and sisters Romans 6:23: "The wages of sin is death, but the gift of God is eternal life in Christ Jesus our Lord."
>
> I was acutely aware of what I was doing. Pregnant with life, I was declaring mortality ("Dust you are and to dust you will return"; Gen. 3:19). I was taking thick black ash and with

¶ For more information on what Lent is and how it's observed, visit tiffanystein.com.

my index finger making the sign of the cross upon each believer's forehead. A declaration for all the world to see—I identify with Christ and with his living, with his dying, and with his rising. And now I enter forty days in the wilderness.

FEBRUARY 2019

JOURNEY TO THE CROSS

Fully God and fully man, Jesus experienced the breadth of human experience. Jesus nursed at the breast of his mother, learned how to walk and talk, and probably grieved the loss of his earthly father. He knew what it was to laugh, cry, enjoy a delicious meal with friends, attend weddings and funerals, and labor at a daily job. Jesus was fully human.

But nowhere is the pain of human life more magnified than during the last week of Jesus' life, when our suffering Messiah headed willingly to the cross and endured the full spectrum of human pain: rejection, goodbyes, betrayal, abandonment, grief, deep sorrow, and anguishing physical harm.

Jesus entered Jerusalem on Sunday to palm branches being waved and shouts of "Hosanna!" and "Blessed is he who comes in the name of the Lord!" and "Blessed is the king of Israel!" (John 12:13). Jesus' disciples believed they were entering Jerusalem for Jesus to be crowned a triumphant king. But Jesus knew better. He knew that the adoration of the crowd would swiftly turn to the sting of violent rejection and that by Friday he would be dead and in a tomb.

Thursday evening Jesus experienced the pain of saying goodbye to people he loved: "It was just before the Passover Festival. Jesus knew that the hour had come for him to leave this world and go to the Father. Having loved his own who were in the world, he loved them to the end" (John 13:1).

Then, while celebrating the Passover meal with his disciples, Jesus became "troubled in spirit and testified, 'Very truly I tell you, one of you is going to betray me'" (John 13:21). Jesus had spent three years in close proximity to and ministry with Judas, and even knowing that the pain of betrayal was imminent, Jesus still chose to humbly wash the dirt-caked feet of and break bread with his betrayer.

After washing the feet of his disciples, eating the Passover meal, and praying for all believers (including you and me), Jesus walked with his disciples to the garden of Gethsemane. And it was there, in the dark, that his love shone most brilliantly. Already carrying the pain of rejection, goodbyes, and betrayal, Jesus pleaded, "Father, if you are willing, take this cup from me; yet not my will, but yours be done" (Luke 22:42). If that isn't an honest prayer, I don't know what is.

Do you want to know who someone truly is? Observe them in crisis. What words seep forth when they're racked with pain and wrestling with a painful reality? What actions do they take when in the pit of despair? Who and what do they turn their attention to when they're alone, betrayed, beaten, mocked, and facing death?

In the dark of night—when no one else was watching, when his beloved friends were sleeping rather than praying with him—Jesus revealed his true nature. He turned his face toward the Father, for the sake of love.

In anticipation of bearing the crushing weight of the entire world's sin and being separated from the Father, Jesus was so "sorrowful and troubled" that he told Peter, James, and John, "My soul is overwhelmed with sorrow to the point of death" (Matt. 26:37-38). Luke records, "And being in anguish, he prayed more earnestly, and his sweat was like drops of blood falling to the ground" (Luke 22:44). In all eternity, Jesus had never been separated from the love and fellowship of the Father.

And while the Father didn't take the cup of suffering from Jesus—reminding us yet again that suffering doesn't indicate the lack of God's love—he did hear his Son and respond with love. Russ Ramsey writes, "This was not a prayer spoken into a void. An angel appeared and began to comfort him, revealing two immovable facts: that the Father cared about his Son's agony so much he would not leave him alone and that the course was set. Jesus would be poured out like Passover wine—emptied until there was nothing left."[9]

Yet, in his great love for us, Jesus continued to the cross, knowing full well the continued horrors that awaited him.

In the hours leading up to his crucifixion, Jesus was intentionally disowned and abandoned in the dark by one of his dearest friends, Peter. He was flogged, mocked, spit upon, taunted, and so physically weak from torture that a bystander was forced to carry his weighty cross up to Golgotha (Luke 23:26). And although Jesus was crucified in the middle of the day, the sky was like night: "From noon until three in the afternoon darkness came over all the land" (Matt. 27:45).

You know what it's like to be in the dark. You're literally without light, without a guide, and without the ability to see and perceive your surroundings. The darkness is a place of disorientation, despair, and hopelessness. It's a place of pain.

Yet Jesus willingly entered the darkness of Good Friday. He didn't just draw near to the cross. He took your place and mine. So great was the pain of eternal separation of humanity from God that God himself chose to become our substitute and bore the pain and punishment in our place (1 Pet. 3:18).

And it is from the depths of that darkness that Jesus cried,

"My God, my God, why have you forsaken me?" (Matt. 27:46). In a statement so mysterious and profound that scholars continue to debate its meaning, Jesus was quoting from Psalm 22: "My God, my God, why have you forsaken me? Why are you so far from saving me, so far from my cries of anguish?" (Ps. 22:1). As scholar R. T. France writes, "this is no dispassionate theological statement, but an agonized expression of a real sense of alienation, reflecting the full meaning of Jesus' death as a 'ransom for many' ([Matt.] 20:28)."[10]

France notes, "This is, remarkably, the only time in the Synoptic Gospels where Jesus addresses God without calling him 'Father.'"[11] Was Jesus dispensing with familial language due to his sense of utter abandonment? Did the struggle to breathe cause him to mince words? Was he so keenly experiencing the burden of sin that shame prevented him from calling God Father? We don't know. But we do know that "Jesus never lost his faith in God."[12] Jesus, the God-man, simply did what we all do in lament. He cried out to the only one who could save him: "*My* God, *my* God" (Matt. 27:46, emphasis mine).

In God's great mystery, death is confronted and defeated upon the cross with a love so powerful that nothing and no one can separate us from it: "I am convinced that neither death nor life, neither angels nor demons, neither the present nor the future, nor any powers, neither height nor depth, nor anything else in all creation, will be able to separate us from the love of God that is in Christ Jesus our Lord" (Rom. 8:38-39).

WHERE IS EASTER?

They say you can trust the man who died for you. And you can. It was for love that Christ laid down his life. But honestly, death isn't the hardest part—the agony comes in waiting to see if there will be a resurrection.

My journal entry continues:

> And now I enter forty days in the wilderness.
>
> And wilderness it was. David was born a week after Ash Wednesday, and he died two weeks after Easter. His life was defined by Lent, except I don't feel like we got to celebrate him. We didn't get Easter, God. Where is Easter?
>
> Lent culminates in Easter. Death is defeated by life. Despair gives way to hope. And what was broken is made new.
>
> But honestly, the past year hasn't been Easter. It's been Lent. We sit in Good Friday, and in the hard, grisly truth that our son is dead. There was no miracle for him. You didn't divinely heal his little body, and you didn't give him a new heart. He didn't get new life. He died. And here I sit, still grieving, still crying out, "Where is your goodness, God?"
>
> FEBRUARY 2019

There is a sacred beauty in a Good Friday service. Often the most somber service of the liturgical year, the universal church gathers to contemplate the cross. At my former church, worship is stripped down to a few stringed instruments and a single voice. The lights are dimmed, the message is simple, and the cross that normally hangs above the stage lies in front of the pulpit, draped in black cloth. At the conclusion of the service, we are invited to file by the cross.

One by one, we run our hands over the rough-hewn planks. We feel the heft of the crossbeam and touch the railroad spikes.

In the absence of sound and light, we leave the sanctuary in silence and darkness.

We, the people of God, are sent out into a lightless world where it's Holy Saturday and Jesus remains dead in the grave.

Yes, there will be an Easter. But not yet. The sun only rises after the darkness of night.

REFLECTION QUESTIONS

1. How would you describe the posture you currently have toward God? Is it one of attack and accusation, curious reciprocity, somewhere in between, or something else entirely?

2. What are some of your first memories of God? Who or what were the primary sources that contributed to your understanding of God? To what degree do you think those sources accurately depicted God?

3. Reflect on the reality that Jesus experienced the full range of human experiences and emotions, including the pain of rejection, goodbyes, betrayal, abandonment, grief, deep sorrow, and physical anguish, all of which he felt in just the last week of his life. How does Jesus' experience speak to your current pain of mourning both something lost and the God you thought you knew?

PRAYER

God, you've revealed yourself to be love, and nowhere is your love more evident than on the cross. And sometimes that feels like enough, but many days, when I'm overwhelmed by my pain and grief, your love still feels far removed. When it feels like Holy Saturday, would you remind me that Easter is coming? I need hope in the darkness. Amen.

For the joy set before him he endured the cross, scorning its shame, and sat down at the right hand of the throne of God. Consider him who endured such opposition from sinners, so that you will not grow weary and lose heart.

HEBREWS 12:2-3

PART 2

darkness

4

Breaking Point: *The Wall*

I have been deprived of peace;
I have forgotten what prosperity is.
Then I thought, "My future is lost,
as well as my hope from the LORD."

Remember my affliction and my homelessness,
the wormwood and the poison.
I continually remember them
and have become depressed.

LAMENTATIONS 3:17-20, CSB

From the moment of our baptism into the death of Jesus,
we begin the practice of dying by degrees—dying to . . . self-centered
pursuits of anything that wars against our vocation as disciples.

DOUGLAS KAINE McKELVEY, *EVERY MOMENT HOLY II*

For a few months after David died, I was okay, and by that I mean I remained busy. Jason and I intricately planned David's memorial service and designed his custom headstone. I created memory books of special moments with David for each of our family members and wrote thank-you notes. We traveled, went to a retreat for grieving parents, and returned to work. Miraculously, the sun still dared to shine each morning, and not knowing what else to do, I numbly resumed the motions of daily life. Eat. Sleep. Clean. Work. Walk the dog. Watch TV. Brush my teeth. Answer emails. Purchase a Costco membership to buy dark chocolate and lotion-infused tissues in bulk.

And then it all fell apart:

> I am angry, and I'm ashamed and mad at myself for being angry. Why? Because I hold the false belief that I'm in control and should be able to regulate all my emotions. That Christians don't experience rage. That mature Christians don't lose control and want to break every drinking glass in their cabinet and delight in the satisfying explosion of glass all over the kitchen floor. I'm those shards. Ragged. Sharp. Blown into a million bits of rubble with a single smash.
>
> What do I grab and hold on to? Is anything sure? Can I count on anything? Will I ever be whole again? Will I always feel so broken, raw, on edge, tender, sensitive, mad, sad, and lost all at the same time? What is normal when you visit your only child in the cemetery? When your beloved baby boy lies in the ground? When your tears fall on dead grass scorched by the hot June sun?
>
> JUNE 2018

I didn't know it then, but I had hit the Wall—a very real place in a believer's growing relationship with God. For some, hitting the Wall is instantaneous, a singular moment in time, equivalent to a car smashing into a concrete barrier at such a high speed that the car warps into a crumpled metal shell. For others, encountering the

Wall is a more gradual experience, like a piñata getting whacked at a birthday party. With each successive smack, the piñata weakens until it finally splits and spills forth its contents.

I became that piñata. David's diagnosis, health challenges, and death initiated my Wall experience, but it was the unrelenting grief tossing me back and forth that wore me down and eventually broke me apart.

CRAWLING OFF THE ALTAR

Together we've explored the disorienting reality of grief, named our complaints and concerns before God in the form of lament, and meditated on what God says about himself. Now comes the hardest part of the grief journey: dying to self and then actively waiting at the Wall for God to bring new life.

In their book *The Critical Journey*, Janet Hagberg and Robert Guelich identify six stages in an individual's spiritual journey. Between stage four (The Journey Inward) and stage five (The Journey Outward) is the Wall, "a face-to-face experience with God and with our own will."[1] Whereas previously you may have been content in your relationship with God and enjoyed serving him (stage three: The Productive Life), you're suddenly dealing with a faith crisis that challenges both your view of God and your view of yourself. The invitation at the Wall is to "move from a posture of knowing [answers] to one of seeking [God's direction]."[2]

But like a physical wall, the Wall is immovable. You cannot go under, over, or around the Wall. Instead, you must go *through* it. And to be clear, the you who emerges on the other side of the Wall isn't the same you who started through it. Why? Because the Wall is a place of surrender where you bring your brokenness and allow yourself, if necessary, to be broken further still. It's the place where true healing can begin, but like in all good resurrection stories, it begins with a death: yours.

The Wall is a season in your spiritual journey when you are called to lay down your will and expectations and allow yourself and your understanding of God to be further refined. This is not daily dying to self, like responding with patience instead of anger when your boss critiques your work or serving in kids' ministry on Sunday mornings when you'd rather be at brunch with friends eating blueberry ricotta pancakes. No, the Wall is a critical, life-altering period marked by the invitation to repeatedly confess, "Not my will, but yours be done" (Luke 22:42).

You may be thinking, *Wait! I've already surrendered my life to Jesus. I'm mad at him and have some questions about who he is, but I'm still a Christian.* And that's correct. You are a Christian, your salvation is secure, and nothing and no one can ever take away your eternal inheritance (Eph. 1:13-14).

But don't forget, child of God, that you're also a living sacrifice (Rom. 12:1). And the problem with living sacrifices—as opposed to truly dead ones—is that they keep crawling off the altar.[3] You may say you want God's will to be done, but often don't you honestly just want God to bless your own will and walk with you as you go your own way? I know I do. The apostle Peter knew that temptation too.

THE WAILING WALL

Peter's résumé is impressive. He was one of the first two disciples called to follow Jesus, and when Jesus approached him, Peter immediately left behind everything—friends, family, livelihood, and home (Matt. 4:18-20). He had the faith to walk on water, was one of the three disciples closest to Jesus, and confessed Jesus as "the Messiah, the Son of the living God" (Matt. 16:16). Peter witnessed the transfiguration of Jesus and heard the Father say, "This is my Son, whom I love; with him I am well pleased. Listen to him!" (Matt. 17:5).

To say Peter knew Jesus is an understatement. Peter walked with Jesus, ate with him, learned from him, and ministered with him for three years. Peter intimately knew Jesus, and Jesus counted him as a close friend. Yet he still got a lot of things wrong about Jesus. Because Peter saw things through the distorted lens of his own desires, he anticipated a victorious Jesus overthrowing the Roman oppressors and setting up a Jewish government.

So when Jesus predicted his own death, Peter quickly rebuked him and said, "Never, Lord! . . . This shall never happen to you!" (Matt. 16:22). To this Jesus replied, "Get behind me, Satan! You are a stumbling block to me; *you do not have in mind the concerns of God, but merely human concerns*" (Matt. 16:23, emphasis mine). When Peter witnessed Elijah and Moses present with Jesus during the transfiguration, he wanted to set up shelters and remain there permanently. And when Jesus predicted that all his disciples would abandon him and that Peter specifically would disown him three times before the rooster crowed, Peter exclaimed, "Even if I have to die with you, I will never disown you" (Matt. 26:35). And Peter tried to make good on that claim. When the Pharisees came to arrest Jesus, Peter attempted to fight them off and ended up slicing off the ear of the high priest's servant. Peter expected Jesus to resist arrest and call down angels to aid him. Instead, Jesus healed the servant's ear and allowed himself to be taken.

We can easily imagine the questions Peter may have asked himself, because they're the type of questions you and I still ask today when wrestling with doubt: What kind of God was Jesus? Wasn't he strong and powerful? Hadn't he said he was the Son of God? Hadn't they all heard the Father's voice affirming him? Jesus had cast out demons, healed lepers, calmed the storm, and raised the dead. And now Jesus was . . . meek and mild? Submitting to a false trial? Refusing to defend himself? It was all too much for Peter, who had risked everything to follow Jesus and be part of his new Kingdom.

Disappointed, confused, and disillusioned, Peter did exactly the thing he said he wouldn't do: He denied Jesus. In the dark of night, he disowned Jesus—his God, his friend, and his rabbi—three times, going so far as to call down curses upon himself and swear, "I don't know the man!" (Matt. 26:74). This suffering savior wasn't the Jesus Peter thought he knew. But then in the early light of dawn, Jesus made eye contact with Peter, and the rooster crowed. Overcome with the weight of his denial, Peter "*broke down* and wept" (Mark 14:72, emphasis mine), and Jesus' prediction proved true: "You're going to *fall to pieces* because of what happens to me" (Matt. 26:31, MSG, emphasis mine). Peter smacked the Wall hard and came face-to-face with death: the death of his hopes, his expectations, his understanding of self, and his understanding of God and his good will. Sound familiar?

Peter's story proves that you and I can love Jesus fervently, walk with him consistently, and still have much to learn, and even unlearn, about God. As C. S. Lewis writes in his conclusion to *The Chronicles of Narnia*, the Christian walk is an invitation to "come further up and further in" to the loving arms of God.[4] And for Peter, that great transformation began with him breaking apart and wailing at the Wall. Our transformation begins there too.

AT THE WALL

In order to move through the Wall, it's helpful to distinguish between what led you to the Wall and what your Wall actually is. All too often we get stuck and waste lots of time and energy looking back at how we got to the Wall instead of responding to the Wall itself. The how is important, but what's more important is acknowledging where you are so you can discern where you want to go from here. Consider these questions:

1. What inciting event(s) or circumstance(s) led you to the Wall?

2. What was lost along the way? Specifically, what are you mourning?

3. What does your Wall experience look and feel like? How is it affecting you spiritually, mentally, emotionally, physically, relationally, and so on? Use your five senses to describe or draw the experience.

4. Now that you're at the Wall, what do you long for or need to move forward? (For example, do you need answers or the presence of a specific person to support you? Are you looking for a detailed plan for what's next or a general direction in which to head? Are you seeking closure, healing, or courage?)

5. From where or whom will the provision of what you need come?

Whatever you feel, whatever your experience, whatever brought you here, the fact is that you're here now—at the Wall, *your* Wall. And like Peter, you have a critical choice to make.

Do you want to move forward?

I'm not asking,

Do others want you to move forward?
Should you move forward?
Do you know how to move forward?
Do you have the energy to move forward?
Is now the time to move forward?

The question is simply this: Do you *want* to move forward? It's the essential question to ask every time an obstacle is hit.

When you feel undone by what you've lost, there is a very real temptation to allow your loss to consume and define you. There is a certain comfort in going back to the *before*, and it's easy to glorify what's been lost, hold fiercely to what could have been, and rehearse what should have been.

For me, to accept such a tragic ending for my son seemed like I'd somehow failed both David and God. My internal storyteller kept trying in vain to rewrite the ending and rearrange all the circumstances for a different outcome. *If we would have tried . . . If I'd just known . . . If only we'd had more time . . .*

But each rewrite was another whack to my metaphorical piñata, reminding me over and over again that I wasn't in control of the storyline.

The only thing I was in control of was my response to the Wall. I didn't want David's life or our family's story to be defined by death. So I vowed that death would claim no more ground in our family and that I would fight death and his comrades of misery, despair, and regret by choosing to live. I also pragmatically reasoned that if I had to hit the Wall and experience the devastating pain of losing both David and the God I thought I knew, then I at least wanted something good—like spiritual growth—to result.

Friend, the worst has happened, and you're experiencing the resulting pain, fallout, and suffering. But this isn't all there is. God invites you to move with him *through* the pain. To move forward is to be a living sacrifice and surrender the hopes of your inner storyteller (bless them!) to the healing journey God desires to take you through (Rom. 12:1). It is a costly journey, but new life is formed in the process. And so Jesus gently asks, "Do you want to get well?" (John 5:6).

Let me say that there's no shame whatever you choose. God loves you no matter what, and nothing you do or don't do could ever change that eternal reality. You are a beloved child of God. Sometimes you may feel too exhausted to try moving forward or feel that you need to build a better support system before engaging in this journey. There may be more urgent needs to attend to, or you may not have a safe space to fall apart. There are hundreds of valid reasons why people decide not to engage with the Wall in their current situation.

But may I encourage you? If you have the slightest inkling, the faintest desire to move forward, why not give it a try? Take a small step, and see where it leads you. Whatever you do, don't let the Wall be a place of passivity, because inaction is also a decision. Actively decide if you're going to move forward, and if not right now, set a date for when you'll revisit your decision. The Wall isn't going anywhere, and the invitation will always be the same: to enter the process of laying down your will, and in the refining, to experience life more abundantly (see John 10:10).

REFLECTION QUESTIONS

1. Take a moment to bring awareness to your mind, body, and soul. On a scale of 1 to 10, with 1 being *Never* and 10 being *I'm ready right now*, how desirous are you to move through the Wall?

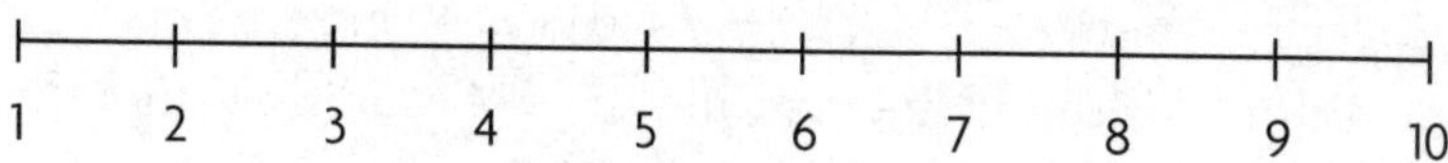

2. What are some of the fears or hesitations you have about engaging with the Wall?

3. What are some of your hopes or desires in engaging with the Wall?

4. What barriers or challenges do you anticipate in engaging with the Wall?

5. What people or resources might assist you in working through those challenges (e.g., a trust friend, a guided retreat, a dedicated space to process, silence and solitude, professional therapy, etc.)?

PRAYER

What decision are you making today? Check the appropriate box, and then pray your own prayer or use the prayer prompt below.

- ☐ **I'm not yet ready to move forward, but I'll revisit on ______________ (date).**

  God, I don't feel ready. This feels too hard, like you're asking too much of me. I'm deeply hurting; you know that. Would you come and comfort me? Grant me the discernment to know when to move forward and the faith to do so (Mark 9:24). Amen.

- ☐ **I'm ready to move forward.**

Consider sharing your decision to move forward with a safe and trusted friend or family member who can encourage you along the way.

God, I'm scared and uncertain as to the outcome, but I want to move forward and work through this pain together. I don't know how to be a living sacrifice and stay on the altar, especially when the suffering depletes me. Please reveal yourself to me and teach me surrender and dependence on you. Grow me, grant me the faith and strength needed for this journey, and increase my trust in you (Ps. 56:3). Amen.

I am sure of this, that he who started a good work in you will carry it on to completion until the day of Christ Jesus.

PHILIPPIANS 1:6, CSB

5

Hold On: *Waiting in the Dark*

How long, LORD? Will you forget me forever?
How long will you hide your face from me?
How long must I wrestle with my thoughts
and day after day have sorrow in my heart?

PSALM 13:1-2

When I hit the Wall, I tried to sprint through it with the sheer propulsive energy of my anger at death. When I wasn't at work, I was diligently engaging with my grief. I read therapeutic books on grief, saw a grief therapist, participated in a GriefShare group, and devoured memoirs of parents who had lost children to learn how they coped. I prayed fervently, journaled everything, ministered to others who were grieving, and tried to share honestly when others asked how I was doing. *Move forward!*

I was doing my part—the hard and painful work of processing grief—and I expected God to do his part as well: show up and bring the healing.

But despite my best efforts to engage with my grief and surrender my disappointments to Jesus, it didn't seem like anything was happening. I didn't feel like I was moving forward. It didn't feel like anyone was listening to my cries. It seemed like no help was coming. That no one was coming.

As the gap between what I thought I needed to move forward and the provision of it widened, I fell into the chasm of desperation. *I am utterly alone.* In my overeager attempt to make it through the Wall, I fell face-first into a Dark Night of the Soul.

THE DARK NIGHT

In the journey of grief, the Wall is inevitable. We all reach a breaking point where we have to decide if we're going to take that next step forward. What comes next, though, is different for everyone. I don't know why. Sometimes God chooses to reveal himself at the Wall and tangibly provides a way through the pain to the other side. But sometimes the provision and presence we so desperately long for and expect don't show up, and we're left feeling like we're groping blindly through a cavernous void. This experience of darkness is called the Dark Night of the Soul.

St. John of the Cross, a sixteenth-century Spanish priest who wrote about the phases of the spiritual life, described a Dark Night as an extended period of time in which God seems absent despite your desire to be with him. Pete Scazzero, author of *Emotionally Healthy Spirituality*, writes, "How do we know we are in 'the dark night'? Our good feelings of God's presence evaporate. We feel the door of heaven has been shut as we pray. Darkness, helplessness, weariness, a sense of failure or defeat, barrenness, emptiness, dryness descend upon us. The Christian disciplines that have served us up to this time 'no longer work.' We can't see what God is doing and we see little visible fruit in our lives."[1]

If any of these things are familiar to you, I'm truly sorry. The Dark Night is a painful, lonely, and disorienting place to be. It's confusing to you—because didn't God promise to be with you always (Heb. 13:5)? And it's confusing to others, because it looks like your faith is flailing and failing. (And isn't it easy to judge others instead of being attentive to our own spiritual lives?)

Let me assure you, the Dark Night resulting from traumatic loss is *not* God punishing you. It's not a result of your sin, and it shouldn't be confused with clinical depression. The Dark Night is simply a season in your relationship with God when he feels distant—absent even.

So if our exploration of the Wall didn't resonate with you—or even felt cruel because the Wall asks you to give still more of yourself when you have absolutely nothing left—perhaps it's because you're in the Dark Night, like I was. And friend, the goal here isn't to move forward. *Thank God!* The invitation is to persevere and hold on tightly as you're bumped and jostled along a road you never desired or expected to take.

A HOLY THIRST

My Dark Night wasn't an impenetrable inky night but a beige wasteland. I told my counselor, Sherry, that I felt like I was in a vast, empty desert. The sand was beige and unbroken, undulating mounds stretching as far as I could see. The sun reflected off the sand, making the dull sky hazy and blinding my eyes. There was no water to be found and no life or signs of life. It was as if I'd been dropped into a barren world of nothingness before day one of creation, when God started bringing order to chaos.

The drab desert would have been more bearable if there were a path or even markers. Even if the path seemed to stretch on forever, at least I would know I was going somewhere, somewhere that would have a destination, an end point. But with no path, no signposts, and no direction as to where to go, any movement felt futile. What if I was headed in the wrong direction or, worse, backtracking? Where was my guide? Where were his fingerprints and direction? What was I supposed to do in this dreary wasteland?

Exhausted by the feeling that I was wandering in circles and wasting my limited time and energy, I was parched for God's presence. And for the first time, I finally understood these words by King David: "You, God, are my God, earnestly I seek you; I thirst for you, my whole being longs for you, in a dry and parched land where there is no water" (Ps. 63:1).

Even though David, described as a man after God's own heart (1 Sam. 13:14), had been anointed as king and sealed with God's divine favor and blessing, he still spent years of his life running from the murderous King Saul and later from his own son. David wrote these words while hiding in the Judean Desert, without food, water, or a comfortable place to rest his head at night. David knew what it was to be in want. And yet what did David want most? God. It was God he most thirsted for.

Frankly, I always thought passages like this one were a bit much—flowery rhetoric from an "extra" person who frequently liked to remind you of his special relationship with God. Surely ordinary people like you and me aren't expected to profusely pine after God like this?

And then I became guilty of it too. Pining. Not in the first-love infatuation sort of way, but in the *Help! Rescue me!* sort of way. When I initially hit the Wall, my cry had been "Heal me, God!" I thought what I most needed was to work through my grief and find a salve for my wounds.

But gradually my cry morphed into "Be with me, God. Show

me your love!" As the painful silence stretched on month after month, I became more desperate to hear from God and feel his presence. If absence makes the heart grow fonder, my desperation for God reached a fever pitch. I realized that I didn't need healing as much as I first needed God. Not the God of my projections or expectations but the real and true God. He was the only one who could sustain me through the loss of my son, the Wall, the Dark Night, and anything else the world might throw at me.

You see, we're rarely thirsty when we have an abundant water supply. We sip so regularly and habitually from our ever-present thermoses that we never actually thirst. It's not until I reach for my water bottle and find it isn't there that I begin to miss it. And the longer I go without drinking, the thirstier I become. As I search for my water bottle, my appreciation for water grows. It's refreshing. It nourishes me. It keeps me alert and thinking clearly. It hydrates my skin. And now I'm not just thirsty; I'm also longing for this mysterious clear liquid that sustains my life.

The Dark Night reveals what we truly thirst for.

Consider how you answered the question "What do you long for or need to move forward?" in the last chapter. Friend, who or what are you truly thirsting for?

Are you longing for closure now that your divorce has been finalized? While hearing from your ex about why your marriage fell apart may be insightful, it won't restore the broken relationship. *Is your deeper thirst to be in a safe, covenantal relationship where you are loved unconditionally, exactly as you are?*

Are you seeking healing after being diagnosed with cancer? Physical healing is indeed a gift from God, but good health is only temporary. *Is what you're truly seeking a world where death has no place and everyone lives a full and abundant life?*

Are you in need of a supportive community who will walk with you through the highs and lows of having a medically fragile child? Friends can carry you through the darkest times, but there will be times when they fail to say or do the right things. *Is what you most need the presence of someone who will never leave or forsake you and who advocates continually on your behalf?*

Are you yearning for direction in a chaotic and unpredictable season? Direction may provide a sense of purpose and grant you momentum for moving forward, but it won't eliminate all the obstacles and challenges you face. *Is what you're truly longing for the assurance that someone is watching out for you and is always working for your good?*

The unique opportunity in the Dark Night is to realize that God's seeming absence is the very thing driving you toward him. *Hold on.* Deprived of all former comforts, pleasures, and distractions, you begin to realize that those things you thought you needed to survive are no longer as essential. There is a reordering of priorities, loves, and needs. And finally, startling clarity comes in the quiet of the Dark Night: When everything else is stripped away, God alone remains. He is all you need. His presence is what you seek.

PETER'S DARK NIGHT

Suffering begs for presence. It pleads, "Will you be with me in this?"

Jesus once asked a similar question to those he loved. After a particularly hard teaching that some found offensive, many disciples "turned back and no longer followed him" (John 6:66). Turning to the twelve disciples, Jesus then asked, "'You do not want to leave too, do you?'. . . Simon Peter answered him, 'Lord, to whom shall we go? You have the words of eternal life. We have come to believe and to know that you are the Holy One of God'" (John 6:67-69).

In other words, Jesus was Peter's only hope. Peter believed that Jesus was the Son of God, and he was committed to suffering with and for Jesus—even vowing to die for him if it came to it (Matt. 26:35).

But Peter failed to grasp one important thing: Jesus wasn't asking him to physically die for him in that exchange. Jesus asked him to trust and follow him (Matt. 4:19), even if things didn't work out as Peter expected. And isn't death to our own will and way sometimes the more painful death?

Peter desperately wanted Jesus to overthrow the corrupt, pagan Roman government and establish an earthly kingdom. Peter was certain of the future and confident of his place in it. But then Peter's hard-fought dream started to fall apart. He denied his Lord three times—not while being tortured or flogged, not while being tried, but simply out of fear of being associated with a failed king.

A few hours later, it was done. Jesus had been brutally crucified and lay dead in a tomb. Peter's wailing at the Wall had morphed into a Dark Night.

Guilt stricken and denied the opportunity to reconcile with Jesus, Peter—I imagine—not only grieved but also felt abandoned by God (which is ironic, since he was the one who had abandoned Jesus). He may have asked, *What was the point of the past three years?* He had left everything behind, *everything*, to help establish Jesus' rule and reign (Luke 5:11). Peter had healed the sick, raised the dead, cleansed those with leprosy, driven out demons, and boldly preached, "The kingdom of heaven has come near" (see Matt. 10:7-8). Where was the Kingdom and its power now? Where was the God he thought he knew? Was this how it all ended—in miserable, embarrassing defeat?

Then, on Sunday morning, Peter and John were informed by a distraught Mary Magdalene that Jesus' body had been taken. *Could it get any worse?*

Peter and John hastily ran to the now-empty tomb, and when they looked in, they saw the neatly wrapped linen and breathed a big sigh of relief; this wasn't a hasty grave robbery. But they may have left the tomb with their faith in divergent places. John saw the empty tomb and believed that Jesus had risen (John 20:8). But what did Peter believe about the empty tomb? Scripture is silent.

Even after the risen Jesus appeared to Peter and the rest of the disciples, "open[ing] their minds so they could understand the Scriptures" (Luke 24:45), Peter may have been uncertain. Who was this "new" Jesus really? What was Peter supposed to do with his own "new" role as one sent out to the world (John 20:21)?

And so, likely pondering these "new" things, Peter returned to what was familiar and comfortable—fishing—and the other disciples decided to join him (John 21:3). They were career fishermen who knew when, where, and how to fish. Yet they caught nothing that night, not a single fish. I wonder if Peter again felt like a failure. *Can't I just get something right?*

Then, early in the morning, an indistinct figure appeared on the shore and encouraged the disciples to try throwing their net to the right side of the boat. With nothing to lose, they did, and their net became so full of fish that they were unable to haul it into their boat. "It is the Lord!" John suddenly exclaimed (John 21:4-7).

Not willing to miss the opportunity to reconcile with Jesus, Peter eagerly swam ashore, where he feasted on the provision of fish and enjoyed the physical presence of Jesus (John 21:7-14). Once again, Jesus asked Peter a heart-penetrating question: "Do you love me?" (John 21:15-17). I'm certain the memory of Jesus asking his disciples "You do not want to leave too, do you?" (John 6:67) echoed in Peter's mind. Peter remembered his urgent proclamation of Jesus as the Messiah, his vow to die for him, and then his failure to be with him in his moment of suffering and his subsequent hiding in the dark. If suffering asks for presence, then Peter had failed Jesus. And so Jesus asked Peter the deeper question: "Do you love me?"

Three times Jesus asked Peter, "Do you love me?" and each time Peter replied with a version of "Yes, Lord, you know that I love you" (John 21:15-17). For three denials there were three declarations of love. But if you think this story is merely about Peter seeking forgiveness and being reconciled to Jesus, you miss a critical point. Peter isn't the main character here. Jesus is.

Jesus' entire relationship with Peter had been about inviting Peter into a deeper relationship with the self-revealing triune God. In fact, right before he had been betrayed by Judas, Jesus had explicitly told his disciples, "I am the way and the truth and the life. No one comes to the Father except through me. If you really know me, you will know my Father as well. *From now on, you do know him and have seen him*" (John 14:6-7, emphasis mine). Our God is a pursuing God who continues to seek us out in love and longs for us to know him more fully.

So how does the Savior of the world conclude his conversation with Peter? "Follow me!" (John 21:19). With a statement from Jesus that is as commanding as it is inviting, Peter is restored and commissioned to shepherd the sheep of God's flock (John 21:15-19). And because you can't follow someone who isn't with you, "Follow me!" is a restatement of Jesus' love for Peter *and* an affirmation of what Peter now realized had always been true: God was present with him. He always had been and always would be (see Deut. 31:6).

Here's what I want us to notice about Peter's Dark Night: God was with him the entire time, but Peter couldn't see it in the moment. Instead, God granted sight to Peter in a gradual and ongoing manner, according to his perfect timing and will.

- Peter didn't initially understand the implications of the empty tomb. The risen Jesus explained the Scriptures to him in light of the resurrection.
- Peter received a personal call from the risen Jesus to be a sent one, but he went back to fishing. Jesus spoke new identity and purpose over him.
- Peter didn't know who called for him to throw his net to the right of the boat after a futile night of fishing, even though an almost identical event had happened just three years prior when Jesus had called Peter to follow him (Luke 5:4-7). Jesus plainly revealed his identity as the victorious King.

Often it's not until you're past the Dark Night that you have the clarity and understanding to look back and see God's fingerprints. *Ahh! There he is!*

While I can't tell you when or how your Dark Night will end, I can assure you that God is with you, just as he was with Peter. You may not see God yet, but he is pursuing you with unfailing love, and one day all will be revealed (Luke 8:17).

So take courage, my friend. Because when you have nothing to give, lack the will to keep going, and are drained of all strength but somehow still breathe, there can be only one conclusion: The mysterious God is sustaining you. He is holding on to you.

May the God who wastes nothing grant you the ability to persevere and hold on. May you have trusted friends in your life who can point to God's goodness and definitively cry, "It is the Lord" (John 21:7), especially when you cannot see him. May the sight of others strengthen and increase your faith. You are not alone.

As your faith is being refined in the fires of suffering, may it prove to be "of greater worth than gold" (1 Pet. 1:6-7). And one day, may you need not ask, "Where are you, God?" or even "Who are you, God?" For by having walked through the fire and endured the Dark Night, you will more clearly know the Lord (John 21:12). He is with you.

And above all else, you are loved (Ps. 136:1).

REFLECTION QUESTIONS

1. If you have experienced or are currently experiencing a Dark Night of the Soul, how would you describe it? What does it look and feel like?

2. If you were to ask a trusted friend or family member how they've seen God at work in your season of suffering, what would they say? (If they're not experiencing the Dark Night of the Soul, they might be able to see something you can't, and their perspective might encourage your heart.)

3. Realistically, what might holding on look like for you in this season?

PRAYER

God, I'm desperate for your presence. I thirst for you but cannot find you anywhere. Sustain me in this desert, in this Dark Night of the Soul. Hold on to me, especially when I struggle to hold on to you. Lead me to the light. Amen.

Give thanks to the Lord, for he is good.
His love endures forever. . . .
to him who led his people through the wilderness;
His love endures forever.

PSALM 136:1, 16

6

Look for God's Goodness: *Hope*

For in this hope we were saved. But hope that is seen is no hope at all. Who hopes for what they already have? But if we hope for what we do not yet have, we wait for it patiently.

ROMANS 8:24-25

And the LORD remembered her.

1 SAMUEL 1:19

Three days after David's death, I opened Facebook Messenger to see a message from a friend of a friend, a complete stranger. It simply said: "I'm sorry for your loss. I have raised people from the dead. If I can have access to David's body, I can raise him, too."

True story. I chose not to engage and deleted the message.[1] Because the only thing worse than David being dead was hoping that he could live again only to discover that he was indeed still dead. No mother should experience the death of her child twice.

Wishes are ubiquitous, desire runs rampant, and goals are the cornerstone of enterprise, but hope? I don't have to tell you that hope is a dangerous thing—a simple four-letter word that packs the same punch as all the other notorious four-letter words when it lets you down. It can seem like a fairy tale made up to ease children's fears at bedtime. And I don't know about you, but when I'm in the depths of suffering, I don't want sugarcoated falsehoods designed to make me feel better temporarily. I need the raw, unvarnished truth.

Thankfully, contrary to the popular misuse of the word, *hope* is defined by *Merriam-Webster* as "desire accompanied by expectation of or belief in fulfillment."[2] That definition is closer to the biblical concept of hope, but the fulfillment part still confuses us—after all, our hopes often do go unfulfilled. And truthfully, when we hope in things, outcomes, or people that can fail, we are inevitably disappointed. We may muster up the courage to hope again and believe things could be better, but the hurt just intensifies when our hopes are dashed once more. It's a vicious cycle that prompts many of us to discard hope as an empty happily ever after. But the problem isn't hope itself—it's who or what we're hoping for.

BIBLICAL HOPE

What is biblical hope? Pastor John Mark Comer defines biblical hope as the "expectation of coming good based on the person and promises of God."[3] This clear, succinct definition highlights the fact that true hope, biblical hope, is based solely on the character of God and is also relational and future oriented.

The fact that hope springs forth from the character of God is a beautiful thing, because hope based on anything imperfect fails. But hope based on the perfect, all-knowing, all-powerful, and all-loving God, whose character is constant and consistent, will be fulfilled. If God says he will do it, he will. If God says it will come to pass, it will. Hope in God provides certainty in a very uncertain world, and isn't that what we all want? To know that a good God is working in all things for his glory and our good (Rom. 8:28), especially when we're at the breaking point or feeling lost and alone in the dark?

You may be thinking, *That all sounds great, but God* has *disappointed me! I feel like he has let me down, and now I'm just trying to slog through the Wall I crashed into.* Or, as in my case, *Not only do I feel like you have let me down, God, but your seeming absence—this aimless wandering in the desert as I cry out for you to reveal yourself—makes my pain more profound! How is hope going to get me through any of this?*

We are called to place our hope in the person and promises of God—in his character—not in a particular outcome or action we long for him to take, no matter how good or right our desire may be. As Comer clarifies, "even when our hope is in Jesus, we often relate to the two disciples on the road to Emmaus; we had *hoped* that Jesus *would do this or that*"[4] (second emphasis mine). Notice the subtle distinction between who Jesus is and what Jesus does. Focusing on the *who* instead of the *what* is why we pray in Jesus' name (John 14:13) and according to his will (1 John 5:14): *I desire this, Lord, but ultimately, I want your will. Have your way with me, and align my will with yours.*

Let me put it this way: If I evaluate the effectiveness of prayer based on whether God says yes to my request, then is my hope in a particular outcome or in God himself? You may say, *God, help me!* but really be saying, *My will be done.* However, if your motive in praying is to grow in intimacy with God and to become more like him, then whatever the outcome of your request, your prayer has been effective. It has "worked" by drawing you closer to the heart of God.

When we desire God's provision more than we long for God himself, we settle for lesser things. Hope is meant to be grounded in relationship with the only one who will truly satisfy our souls. According to psychiatrist Curt Thompson, "Hope is actually a word that, in the world of interpersonal neurobiology, serves as a proxy for an ever-deepening attachment love with Jesus and the commensurate awareness of God's relational presence of loving-kindness."[5] In other words, the more deeply you come to know the true character of Jesus, the better you will be able to receive, understand, and reciprocate his love.

And why is it important to understand that hope is future oriented? As believers living between the two comings of Christ, we live in the already-and-not-yet period of church history. Jesus has *already* ushered in the Kingdom of God with his death and resurrection, thereby breaking the power of sin and death. That is our present reality. But Jesus has *not yet* returned to put away evil once and for all—our future reality. In that respect, hope is a belief about the future that we practice and live into today. We are able to persevere and hold on in this in-between time, in the present, because we know how the story ends:

> I heard a loud voice from the throne saying, "Look! God's dwelling place is now among the people, and he will dwell with them. They will be his people, and God himself will be with them and be their God. 'He will wipe every tear from their eyes. There will be no more death' or mourning or crying or pain, for the old order of things has passed away."
>
> He who was seated on the throne said, "I am making everything new!" (Rev. 21:3-5)

Truly, *the best is yet to come.*

HANNAH'S HOPE

If ever there was someone I identified with in the Bible, it's Hannah. Her story of persistent faith and expectant hope in God in the midst of deep pain (1 Sam. 1:1–2:11) had always given me encouragement in trying times. But it wasn't until Jason and I lost David, were then diagnosed with secondary infertility, and spent eighteen months trying to conceive another child that I truly understood Hannah's deep longing—no, *need*—for a child.[6]

Hannah lived at the time in Israel's history when the period of the judges had ended and the monarchy was about to begin. In a society where children ensured the longevity of your family name and ancestral lands, provided for your financial future, and cared for you in your old age, to be without children was to be without a future.

Hannah and her husband, Elkanah, desperately longed to have children, but they were unable to conceive. Perhaps for this reason, Elkanah took a second wife at the same time, Peninnah, and had children with her. It seems that Elkanah loved Hannah more than Peninnah, and the jealous second wife provoked and ridiculed Hannah. Peninnah constantly reminded Hannah of the fact that she didn't have children and shamed her for being barren and unable to fulfill her familial role.

After one particularly bitter verbal attack by Peninnah, Hannah went to the Tabernacle, God's dwelling place, and prayed a broken and desperate prayer:

> Oh, God-of-the-Angel-Armies,
> If you'll take a good, hard look at my pain,
> If you'll quit neglecting me and go into action for me
> By giving me a son,
> I'll give him completely, unreservedly to you.
> I'll set him apart for a life of holy discipline.
> (1 Sam. 1:11, MSG)

Hannah's story begins with a deep need and desperate longing for a child. Hannah doesn't stifle her tears, stuff down her hurt, or pretend to have it all together. Instead, she comes just as she is into God's presence, mess and all. She laments and weeps many tears. She prays out of her deep hurt. And she trusts that God is big enough to handle it all.

Lament prayers might feel reasonable, but to dare to ask God for something? Doesn't it feel bold and risky to be so vulnerable? What if you're disappointed yet again?

GOD'S GOODNESS

I was one year into my grief journey when I read these words in the Psalms:

> I would have despaired had I not believed that I would
> see the goodness of the LORD
> In the land of the living.
>
> Wait for and confidently expect the LORD;
> Be strong and let your heart take courage;
> Yes, wait for and confidently expect the LORD.
> (Ps. 27:13-14, AMP)

The New International Version translates that first verse as "I *remain confident* of this: I will see the goodness of the LORD in the land of the living." The Christian Standard Bible states, "I am *certain* that I will see the LORD's goodness in the land of the living" (emphases mine). At the time, I was struggling to find anything worthy of my hope, and the words *confident* and *certain* scared me. Confidence and certainty are absolutes—you either have all of it or none of it. To be *somewhat* certain is not to be certain at all. If you're only *mildly* confident, your belief is tentative at best.

But *despair*? Now that was a solid, weighty word with which I was well acquainted.

Sensing that I was in good company with King David, who also intimately knew the loss of an infant son (2 Sam. 12:15-23), I was intrigued by his statement that belief in God's goodness was the antidote to the despair I was experiencing. I didn't yet believe wholeheartedly. I wasn't confident, certain, or sure of who God truly was. But I did see a promise that, if true, my life could be reoriented around: "I will see the goodness of the LORD in the land of the living."

Either God was good, and he was going to show me his goodness during my earthly life, or he was not. I sensed an invitation: to take God at his word and to pray for eyes to see his goodness in my life. I intellectually knew that God's goodness didn't equate to assurances that he'd take away my grief, grant me another child, or heal me from chronic depression, although I desperately prayed for each of those things.

Instead, I tried to be realistic about what I was looking for by listing what God's goodness to me might look like according to how he's revealed himself in Scripture and in the person of Jesus. On a piece of card stock, I printed the word *EXPECTANT* at the top and then wrote:

I will see the goodness of the Lord in 2019.

- You are for me.
- You will carry me.
- You will continue to prove yourself trustworthy.

- You always have been and always will be with me.
- You will bring life and flourishing in your way at your appointed time.
- You will show me your loving-kindness.
- You will grow in me dependence upon you.
- You are not done working and will give me the strength to wait.

JANUARY 2019

I put the fuchsia card in the front of my Bible and felt a small flicker of hope. I had asked God to show me his goodness—to show me who he truly was—and according to his Word, he was going to do it. Whatever the outcome, I felt certain that by engaging in the process of actively looking for God's goodness I'd better understand the mysterious figure sitting across from me in counseling.

My question was no longer *Is God present in my suffering?* Because if I took God at his word, and that was the hypothesis I was testing, he'd promised to walk with me through the valley of deep darkness—the very valley of life shrouded in death's shadows (Ps. 23:4). God was with me. And so my question took a new, risky form: *God, will you show your love and goodness to me in my suffering?*

HOPE BIRTHED IN SUFFERING

Little did I understand then that Hannah and I were each actively engaged in the formation of durable hope. For some reason, I thought hope was a spiritual gift, like if I prayed hard enough, the Holy Spirit would just give me sustaining hope. But as Curt Thompson observes, "Hope is, perhaps surprisingly, something one *forms*. . . . It is something that only ever becomes durable through the course of suffering."[7] And in that respect, the cultivation of hope turns out to be much like that of patience—a fruit of the Spirit I earnestly desire while also dreading the hard work necessary to develop it.

Well-meaning Christians regularly joke, "Don't pray for patience. God just might give you opportunities to practice it." And if we're honest, God's role in forming virtues like patience and hope can feel a bit suspect, right? But thankfully, not all popular sayings are true. God isn't sitting on the clouds doling out suffering like cheap candy on Halloween night: "Here you go, kids. You get trauma, and you get poverty, and you get shame. Be sure to develop hope with what I've given you. You're welcome!"

To be clear, God is a good God, and he is *not* the author of evil (1 John 1:5). While God does allow suffering—which is an inextricable part of the broken world we live in, as well as sometimes a result of our own choices—he doesn't perpetuate it. He redeems it!

Well acquainted with suffering himself, Paul writes in Romans 5:3-5, "Not only so, but we also glory in our sufferings, because we know that suffering produces perseverance; perseverance, character; and character, hope. And hope does not put us to shame, because God's love has been poured out into our hearts through the Holy Spirit, who has been given to us."[8]

If not suffering, then what have we been gifted by God? A hope that won't disappoint, because it is based solely on the person and promises of God. The person of God—Father, Son, and Spirit, three in one—gives and keeps on giving because of his great love for us. The Father created Adam and Eve in his image and invited them into an intimate relationship with him; the Son gave his own life on the cross; the Holy Spirit has given us himself, the literal indwelling of God.

So you see, hope isn't something you must somehow manufacture on your own. It's not formed in isolation by the power of your own strength in an attempt to just grin, bear it, and get through it. Hope is actually "something we form in response to the loving presence of someone else."[9] In other words, hope can only be constructed in the crucible of suffering when love is present.

LACK, LIMITS, AND LONGINGS

One of the many reasons hope can feel so daunting is because we often struggle to feel, much less see, God's love in our most profound pain. Besides the fact that, biologically speaking, trauma interrupts the integration of the mind and makes love more difficult to perceive and receive, we're also all victims of the telephone game. You know the one—the game where everyone stands in a line, you whisper a sentence in the first kid's ear, he whispers it to the next kid, and so on until the last kid says the sentence aloud. Somewhere along the way, things are misheard or misunderstood, get repeated, and get misunderstood again, and suddenly "Jesus rose from the dead" becomes "Kanye loves bread."

Sometimes our understanding of God goes through this same process. Whether knowingly or unknowingly, our churches, families, schools, authority figures, and neighborhoods have all represented and imaged God to us. Some representations have been more faithful and truer than others. In many cases, the message may have started out as gospel truth, but because something other than Jesus got added along the way, we received garbled good news and a god unworthy of worship. We all end up with an incomplete and flawed understanding of God to some degree, me included.

That distorted image of God makes it difficult sometimes to

recognize his love amid suffering. As Paul writes in 1 Corinthians 13:12, "now I know in part," but when Christ comes, "then I shall know fully, even as *I am fully known*" (emphasis mine).

Paradoxically, it is the unfinished, progressive nature of our faith that invites a living, breathing relationship with God. Think about it. When life is going well and everything seems to be going according to your plan (when you feel in control), it's easy to hold God at arm's length and only consult him on an as-needed basis. When God operates according to your expectations for him, it's easy to mistake your partial knowing and understanding of him as full and complete understanding of him. (Guilty as charged!)

But when suffering comes, you must contend with the brutal reality of lack. You aren't in control and never have been. You're not self-sufficient, God is not beholden to your will, and there is still much you don't understand about God, his will, and his ways.

And it is in this very place, where shame, anger, and disconnection might flourish, that God reveals a better way. As counterintuitive as it may seem, your lack is not a liability but a God-given limit that invites you to "seek the Lord while he may be found; call on him while he is near" (Isa. 55:6). God may have disappointed you, but your lack exposes your need for him all the same. And God meets you in your longing.

As you become less self-reliant and gain greater awareness of your need for God, you have the opportunity to better know God as he is, not as you wish him to be (see Col. 3:9-10). The potential exists for you to develop deeper intimacy with him as you learn to place more and more confidence in the person of God and allow him to grow you in his image.

That's exactly what happened to Hannah.

FORMING HOPE

In a world full of haves and have-nots, power differentials matter. And Hannah *had not.* She was female, childless, mercilessly taunted by her husband's second wife, who did have children, and dependent upon a priest to mediate between her and God. Hannah lived in lack.

Scripture sets up the priest Eli as a direct contrast to Hannah. Eli *had* everything. He was male in a patricentric world, he had at least two sons, and as a priest he possessed religious authority, spoke for God, and enjoyed financial stability and social respectability. The readers of 1 Samuel would expect Eli to be the recipient of God's blessings and favor.

But notice how God flips the cultural narrative. It is not the strong, successful, and self-sufficient who thrive in God's Kingdom but the weak, powerless, and hopeless.

Remember that it was Hannah's lack, or vulnerability, that led her to the Lord. If Hannah hadn't lacked a child, she wouldn't have petitioned God so repeatedly and earnestly. And her longing for God gave her the courage to stand up to Eli when he condemned her falsely and publicly as a drunkard for her prayers.

In her conversation with Eli, Hannah humbly exhibited a personal knowledge of God and his character. She knew the truth! She knew that God was for people exactly *like her*: the marginalized, the forgotten, the overlooked, the misunderstood, and the mistreated. In fact, she later prayed,

> "The bows of the warriors are broken,
>   but those who stumbled are armed with strength.
> Those who were full hire themselves out for food,
>   but those who were hungry are hungry no more.

She who was barren has borne seven children,
  but she who has had many sons pines away.

"The LORD brings death and makes alive;
  he brings down to the grave and raises up.
The LORD sends poverty and wealth;
  he humbles and he exalts.
He raises the poor from the dust
  and lifts the needy from the ash heap;
he seats them with princes
  and has them inherit a throne of honor.

"For the foundations of the earth are the LORD's;
  on them he has set the world." (1 Sam. 2:4-8)

We're not told Eli's thought process. We don't know if he felt defensive, embarrassed, or repentant when corrected by Hannah. But we do know that Eli's posture and tone shifted: "Go in peace, and may the God of Israel grant you what you have asked of him" (1 Sam. 1:17).

According to the *Lexham Bible Dictionary*, *peace* "carries the fundamental meaning of welfare, prosperity, or wholeness as well as the absence of hostility. . . . The term is frequently used as the antithesis of harm . . . and as a synonym for what is good."[10] If you've ever heard someone say, "Shalom," you were hearing the Hebrew word for "peace." Using it when talking to someone means that you desire well-being for that person, and that's exactly what Eli was speaking over Hannah: God's goodness.

In his loving-kindness, God met Hannah in her longing. God spoke to Hannah through Eli—though flawed, Eli still served as a mediator between God and his people—and reminded her that she was seen. She was known, *fully known*. She was able to leave this interaction "no longer downcast" (1 Sam. 1:18), "her face radiant" (1 Sam. 1:18, MSG), not because she'd been promised a child but because she recognized the presence of God's love in her suffering.

WHAT AM I REMEMBERING?

Some things in life are circuitous. And I find that both deeply frustrating and confusing. I don't want to revisit the same places or issues repeatedly. I don't want to find myself back where I started. I want to go to counseling, work through an issue, and know it's resolved. I want to have the hard conversation and move on. I want my life to move forward, preferably up and to the right. In essence, I want the clarity and ease of defined beginnings, middles, and ends.

Frankly, hope can feel a bit circuitous too. If hope is "something we form in response to the loving presence of someone else,"[11] what happens when I don't feel God's loving presence? Can I still form hope? And furthermore, don't I need hope to sustain and motivate me to keep searching for God's loving presence amid suffering when he feels distant—which then is supposed to lead to the formation of hope? Which comes first? The recognition of God's love, which leads to hope—or hope, which leads to the recognition of his love?

Yes. Yes to both.

You see, it was God's loving presence that led Hannah to depart Shiloh in hope. Yet Hannah wouldn't have come to God in the first place if she hadn't already had some hope in him. If Hannah hadn't already trusted God to some degree and thought there was something in his character that might incline him to listen and respond to her, then there wouldn't have been any point in beseeching him to begin with.

Hope, thankfully, is not all or nothing. It exists on a spectrum and can be diminished or increased. And just like with anything else that is formed, there are things you can do in cooperation with the Holy Spirit to enlarge your hope.

It all begins with asking, *What am I remembering?* Curt Thompson explains, "What we pay attention to, we remember. And what we remember becomes our anticipated future."[12] In other words, hope is based on remembrance.

Think of a toddler who is told that tomorrow is Christmas. If they've never experienced Christmas before or can't remember it, that word doesn't mean a whole lot to them. You can describe icicle lights, presents under the tree, delicious snickerdoodle cookies, and family coming over for a meal, but honestly, it's all theoretical at that point—especially for young children, who don't yet have a lot of memories to draw from and are trying to piece together what the day could be like based on their limited experiences.

But you can be sure that after all the sugar and presents of Christmas Day, every day for a week thereafter they'll ask, "Is it Christmas yet?" (Since time is clearly a construct created by parents to frustrate their children and delay their gratification, toddlers everywhere unite in protest by asking, "Is it now? Now? Now?!")

Why the persistent asking? Because they've concretely experienced something very good. They now remember Christmas vividly and can't wait to experience it again—preferably *now*!

We're no different. We're just kids who've grown older, and it's still hard to imagine what we haven't experienced, isn't it?

Perhaps you feel like you haven't experienced God's goodness in a while. But have you experienced God's goodness in the past, at any point, in any way? Remember that today.

As you grow in your ability to *remember* and *rehearse* God's goodness and love in your past, it will become easier to *recognize*

God's goodness and love with you today and to *rely* upon, or anticipate, his good and loving presence in the future.

And friend, you don't have to do the work of remembering and rehearsing alone. Jesus told his disciples, "The Advocate, the Holy Spirit, whom the Father will send in my name, will teach you all things and will *remind* you of everything I have said to you" (John 14:26, emphasis mine). The Father sent the Holy Spirit to remind you of who Jesus is and what he has said and done. In God's triune love, he foresaw your desperation, despondency, and doubt. So God himself reminds you of who he is and what he's done on your behalf.

But there's a truth even more important than your remembrance of God's goodness and love. We see it in God's response to Hannah's prayer: "And the Lord remembered her" (1 Sam. 1:19).

God remembers you.

There have been and will continue to be times when you cannot see God in the midst of pain, cannot summon the energy to look for him, are crushed with depression, or are busy with distraction. Your wavering ability to remember doesn't change the reality that God always remembers.

His remembering evokes action on your behalf. He is present. *And he has remembered you* (see Isa. 49:13-16).

* * *

It was a Saturday afternoon about six months after David died, and I needed a nap. The cold and dreary Portland-esque weather outside my window was compounding my grief and magnifying my fatigue. It had rained for weeks, I was stuck inside, and I sorely missed the sun. I pulled up the goose-down comforter, took one last look outside, and fell asleep to the hisses and howls of the storm.

But when I woke up a few hours later, it was if I had woken up in an entirely different season. Fall was gone, and spring was here. Sun was streaming in through the wall of windows, the sky was clear, and the air was warm. Everything was bright. Colors were intense, and the earth was freshly bathed in sparkling raindrops.

I walked into the living room and commented to Jason, "It's so good to see the sun. It reminds me that there won't always be storms. Eventually the sun will come out." And then I realized that this wasn't just a physical description of my surroundings. It was a specific reminder of God's love for me: *Tiffany, you won't always be in a stormy season. One day the clouds will break and the sun will come shining in.*

And it could happen just like that for you, too. You could go to sleep in the storm and wake up to the sun.

After all, as Anne Lamott observes, "Hope begins in the dark."[13]

REFLECTION QUESTIONS

Use the following questions to help you *remember* and *rehearse* God's goodness and love in your past, even if his goodness is difficult to *recognize* and *rely on* today.

1. In what ways has God carried you through past trials and painful seasons (see Isa. 43:1-3)?

2. How has God displayed his loving-kindness toward you and your family (see Ps. 117:2)?

3. Where has God brought healing and newness of life to broken places in your life (see Ps. 147:3)?

4. How has God provided for your needs (emotionally, spiritually, physically, relationally, etc.)? (See Ps. 23:1.)

5. How have you seen God free you from the grip of sin and grow you in the fruit of the Spirit (see Gal. 5:22-23; 1 Pet. 2:24)?

6. Where have you seen God act on your behalf in ways that couldn't be explained otherwise (see Ps. 34:4-8)?

PRAYER

God, I want to remember and recognize your love and goodness. I want to rely on your love and be a person of hope. But I'm still relearning who you are, and to be hopeful feels risky when your love feels distant. Would you show me your goodness, today, in the land of the living? Amen.

The Lord is good,
a refuge in times of trouble.
NAHUM 1:7

7

The One Who Speaks with You: *Presence*

"Never will I leave you;
never will I forsake you."
HEBREWS 13:5

If you've been there, you know—the hospital waiting room is its own kind of hell. No one has answers, timely updates aren't forthcoming, the TV is stuck on infomercials, the fluorescent lights blink haphazardly, and the coffee is somehow both weak and bitter. But worst of all, you're separated from your loved one for an indeterminate amount of time.

David's NICU was a graveyard of isolation. Because when medically fragile infants occupy the liminal space between life and death, the introduction of visitors and their pathogens creates imminent danger. As a result, only two people could be in David's room at a time, and one of them had to be a parent. If Jason and I both wanted to be with David, no other family member or friend could visit. If one of them wanted to be with David, one of us had to walk out of his room—out of his presence. We had to bear the pain of separation from our son and step into the dreaded waiting room.

We were created for continuous, unbroken relationships. You and I both know it. We feel it in the torment of waiting rooms, the drama of divorce court, and the tearful goodbyes of high school graduations. Whether you're dealing with a literal or metaphorical death, it remains true: Death is life interrupted. It ruptures relationships, it prevents presence, and after the final heartbeat, there remains silence.

I don't know the specific form of silence you're currently facing. I don't know if you're waiting for God to speak, a dream to come to fruition, or a relationship to be reconciled. Honestly, you could be waiting for a long time. But I do know that when you can't see or hear God, you can receive the provision of what he's already shared.[1] In the silence you can return to what he's already spoken.

So before we explore in the Bible God's provision for those in the waiting room, let's start with prayer.

> *Father, I confess that I'm searching—searching for you, your truth, your presence, and your love and goodness. I've hit my breaking point, and I want to move forward. I want to dare to hope again, even in the dark, where you feel distant. I want to believe that, based on your character and promises, good is coming. Would you grant me "clarity to know the truth" and "courage to face the truth and to move forward?"[2] Please impart to me sustaining faith and give me eyes to see you and ears to hear you, especially in the silence. Amen.*

PRESENCE IN THE SILENCE

We're not told what the disciples did on the Saturday their Savior lay in the tomb. We're not told what Mary and Martha did while Lazarus's body decomposed for four days because their Teacher hadn't come to heal their brother. We're not privy to the thoughts, feelings, experiences, or griefs of any of these people. But we know that they, too, were in the waiting room, separated from the ones they loved and submerged in silence.

And we also know that God's silence was not forever.

If God's silence has you worried, take heart. His silence is just for a season. In fact, God's silence in the Bible is often followed by manifestations of his divine presence and a more thorough understanding of him, our loving God.

For hundreds of years, the enslaved Israelites cried out to God for deliverance from the Egyptians (Exod. 2:23). They were worked ruthlessly, subjected to harsh labor, and beaten, and their baby boys were drowned in the Nile in an attempt at population control (Exod. 1:11-16). Why God allowed them to suffer so long we're not told. If God spoke to the Israelites during their enslavement, it isn't recorded. But when God did speak, he declared, "I have heard the groaning of the Israelites, whom the Egyptians are enslaving, and I have remembered my covenant" (Exod. 6:5). What followed was God's greatest act of rescue and redemption prior to Jesus' death on the cross: the exodus.

Then, between the events recorded at the conclusion of the Old Testament and the beginning of the New Testament, there was a four-hundred-year period of "silence" during which no Scripture was recorded. Was God at work and present among his people? Certainly. But the Israelites were still waiting for an Elijah-like figure to come and prepare the way for the soon-coming Messiah (Mal. 4:5). Imagine Zechariah's surprise when, after four hundred years of his ancestors waiting, praying, and longing for a redeemer, he was told he would have a son in his old age who would "make ready a people prepared for the Lord" in "the spirit and power of Elijah" (Luke 1:17). God was speaking again to his people.

DEAD BUT NOT SILENT

We expect God to speak through the life of his Son, Jesus, but what about Jesus' death and the seeming silence of the grave?

There are many places in Scripture where God the Father appears to be silent, but Jesus' death on Good Friday is not one of them. The darkness of the tomb shows us that God speaks in mysterious and unexpected ways. And sometimes God doesn't use words at all to convey his message.

After Jesus cried out and committed his spirit to the Father, he died (Matt. 27:50). And the Father responded to Jesus' death with a cacophony of supernatural works that testified to Jesus' divine sonship and the monumental significance of him laying down his life (John 10:17-18). The Temple curtain, which separated God's dwelling place in the Holy of Holies from the rest of the sanctuary, was "torn in two from top to bottom" (Matt. 27:51). The massive, heavy curtain—estimated to be sixty feet high and thirty feet wide—being torn from top to bottom indicates that God initiated the action, and it attests to his redeeming power (Heb. 10:19-20).[3]

There was an earthquake, rocks split, and the tombs of saints opened, all declaring the power of God over death and the grave (Matt. 27:51-52). These cataclysmic events, along with midday darkness, were so powerful that when the Roman centurion guarding Jesus witnessed them he exclaimed, "Surely he was the Son of God!" (Matt. 27:54). God was speaking.

And after the sound of fabric ripping, boulders tumbling, professional soldiers professing, and stones splitting, there was the grinding of a single large stone being hurriedly rolled in front of the entrance to a tomb (Matt. 27:59-60). It was Friday evening, and the God-man, who had spent decades cutting and carving rock, now lay in a rough-hewn tomb cut by calloused hands like his own.[4] It was dark. And because everyone had rushed home to observe the Sabbath, it was also silent.

Of the four Gospel writers, Matthew is the only one to mention the events of Saturday. He records in Matthew 27:62-66:

> The next day, the one after Preparation Day, the chief priests and the Pharisees went to Pilate. "Sir," they said, "we remember that while he was still alive that deceiver said, 'After three days I will rise again.' So give the order for the tomb to be made secure until the third day. Otherwise, his disciples may come and steal the body and tell the people that he has been raised from the dead. This last deception will be worse than the first."
>
> "Take a guard," Pilate answered. "Go, make the tomb as secure as you know how." So they went and made the tomb secure by putting a seal on the stone and posting the guard.

The Pharisees' mock trial and execution of Jesus was an attempt to publicly humiliate, discredit, and gag the "KING OF THE JEWS" (Matt. 27:37). They wanted Jesus permanently silenced. And by demanding a guard at the tomb, the Pharisees sought to keep him dead. They wanted Jesus' body to be inaccessible to his followers. But their attempts to silence Jesus and ensure his absence that Saturday only made his voice that much louder. For what they failed to recognize is that God had already spoken, was still speaking, and would continue to speak to his people:

> In the past God *spoke* to our ancestors through the prophets at many times and in various ways, but in these last days he has *spoken* to us by his Son, whom he appointed

> heir of all things, and through whom also he made the universe. The Son is the radiance of God's glory and the exact representation of his being, sustaining all things by his powerful *word*. (Heb. 1:1-3, emphasis mine)

God ultimately answered questions about his seeming absence and silence with the living, dying, and rising of his Son, the Word. "The Word became flesh and dwelt among us. We observed his glory, the glory as the one and only Son from the Father, full of grace and truth" (John 1:14, CSB).

Which leads us to ask, *If God is constantly with us, as he promises, and the Father speaks through his Son, the indwelling Holy Spirit, and the Bible, why don't we always hear God's voice and feel his nearness?*

PRESENT OR OMNIPRESENT?

In its most basic sense, God's presence is "God's initiative in encountering people."[5] But complications, confusion, and hurt arise when we mistake God's omnipresence for his manifest presence.

So what is the difference? One writer describes it this way: "God's *omnipresence* means He is always there—even when the awareness is not. His Holy Spirit indwells believers at all times. God's *manifest presence*, however, is something that occurs in our lives as He chooses to reveal Himself. It is something that is sometimes experienced and other times not."[6]

You and I serve a personal God who has made and continues to make himself known. But that gift is also the pain point. You always get God in the sense that he is everywhere at all times; he is omnipresent. But you don't always get to experience God's active, noticeable, and revelatory presence: his manifest presence. "At the times of His choosing, the Spirit manifests His presence, and our theological knowledge becomes an experiential knowledge. Creedal acquaintance becomes loving familiarity. . . . The whole point of God's manifest presence is that our awareness of Him is awakened."[7]

Obviously, Jesus is the full and manifest presence of God because he is God himself (Col. 2:9). But in addition to Jesus, we see God's manifest presence all throughout Scripture:

- God calling Abram to go to a new land (Gen. 12:1)
- God promising Hagar that her offspring would be too many to count (Gen. 16:10)
- God appearing to Moses in a burning bush (Exod. 3:2-3)
- God leading the Israelites in a pillar of cloud by day and a pillar of fire by night (Exod. 13:21)
- God revealing himself to Elijah in a gentle whisper (1 Kings 19:12-13)
- God appointing Jonah to call the Ninevites to repentance (Jon. 1:1-2)
- God sending an angel to tell Mary that she would bear the Son of God (Luke 1:35)
- God gifting the Holy Spirit to the gathered believers at Pentecost (Acts 2:2-4)
- God meeting Saul (Paul) on the road to Damascus (Acts 9:3-6)
- God granting John a vision of the Kingdom (Rev. 1:10-13)

It would be easy to assume that God only reveals himself to those who are worthy, but consider Jonah. Not only did Jonah not want to hear from God, but he ran the other direction when God did speak, and he continued to be full of ethnic hatred (Jon. 1:3; 3:10–4:1).

Nor does God only speak to those who already know him. Abram worshiped pagan gods before God divinely revealed himself (Josh. 24:2).

Nor does God only speak to those who are actively seeking him. Moses was tending sheep when he encountered God in the burning bush (Exod. 3:1-2).

Nor does God only speak to those willing to be led. The Israelites grumbled, complained, rebelled, and accused God of bringing them to the desert to die (Exod. 14:11).

Nor does God only speak to people of significance. Mary was a poor female Israelite teenager from an obscure town, which made her forgettable in the eyes of society (Luke 1:26-27).

When I think of these people, I think, *Why, God? If you chose to reveal yourself to them, why won't you reveal yourself to me? I need you to show up and speak.* Which, if I'm honest, only betrays my sense of self-righteousness and the false belief that I can somehow control or earn God's manifest presence by being good enough (or suffering enough).

The truth is that God's ways are mysterious. His timing and will are not the same as our own, and we don't know why God chooses to manifest his presence in our lives at some times and not others. I don't know why God chose not to show up in the ways you and I expected when we needed him most. To offer conjectures would be nothing but speculation and, ultimately, unhelpful.

But this I know: "Much of the [Old Testament] discussion of the presence of God centers on the fact that God is utterly free to be where God wills but constantly chooses to be with His people to give them life."[8] Don't miss that. Both God's omnipresence and his manifest presence are gifts, freely given, not earned. And his purpose in being present with and dwelling within you is to give *you* life (see John 5:21).

You may not see or feel God's presence. Life may feel a million miles away. But that doesn't mean life isn't being formed within you.

DRAW NEAR

Let's go back to our friends Mary and Martha. Even after they sent for Jesus, telling him his dear friend Lazarus was sick, Jesus delayed traveling to Bethany for two days. And Lazarus died. When Jesus did finally arrive, Lazarus had already been in the tomb for four days (John 11:1-17).

We're rarely granted the full picture of our circumstances. We can't see our loss through the eyes of bystanders, we can't feel it through the hearts of those closest to us, and we certainly can't understand it from the mind of God. But as we read John 11, as we look again at Mary and Martha's grief over the death of their brother, we're given the perspective of at least seven different people. And what we overwhelmingly see is that, despite Mary and Martha's grief that Lazarus died and Jesus was absent when they most wanted him present, *Jesus drew near.*

- *Jesus drew near even when the cost was high.* The decision to go to Bethany to be with Lazarus and his family put Jesus directly in harm's way. When Jesus told his disciples that they would be going back to Judea, they replied, "But Rabbi . . . a short while ago the Jews there tried to stone you, and yet you are going back?" (John 11:8). Jesus willingly went to Bethany ready to lay down his life in order to raise up the life of another. And the disciples' concerns proved true. Because Jesus called Lazarus back to life, the Pharisees plotted to kill Jesus (John 11:53).

- *Jesus drew near emotionally.* Some branches of Christianity teach that you should be happy, or at least content, always. Any emotion falling below neutral is deemed negative and inappropriate for a believer who is filled with the "joy of the Lord" (Neh. 8:10). Yet Jesus was a man who exhibited the full range of emotions, including frustration, anger, and profound grief (Mark 9:19; John 2:13-17).

  When confronted with the death of a loved one, Jesus wasn't stoic, detached, or aloof. He was present. Present to the people, to the place, and to the predicament. The situation so deeply moved and troubled his spirit that the God-man shed tears: "When Jesus saw her weeping, and the Jews who had come along with her also weeping, he was deeply moved in spirit and troubled. 'Where have you laid him?' he asked. 'Come and see, Lord,' they replied. Jesus wept" (John 11:33-35).

  And later, when confronted with his own death, the God-man, "being in anguish," sweat like he was sweating drops of blood (Luke 22:44). Sweat, blood, and tears falling to the ground. Is there anything more human?

  Author and illustrator Scott Erickson says it best:

  > I'm a Christian because of the resurrection, but I'm also a Christian because of the shortest verse in the Bible: "Jesus wept" (John 11:35).
  >
  > If the story of God incarnating into a human life didn't involve him crying at his friend's funeral, then I wouldn't believe it. Because I've cried at my friend's

> funeral—and you have, too—and it would mean that God was insulated from one of the hardest aspects of our human existence: our fragile mortality.[9]

God incarnate. He weeps with us. He weeps for us. He weeps because he personally knows and has now experienced the devastation of death.

- *Jesus drew near to meet others in their pain.* If death is the unraveling of life, then Jesus met Mary and Martha in the fray. After speaking with her, Jesus asked Martha to deliver a message to Mary: "The Teacher is here and is calling for you" (John 11:28, CSB). And Jesus extends the same invitation to you: "I am calling for you."

  Jesus is calling for you. Let that sink in for a minute. Jesus is not calling just *to you* but *for you.* In your pain, in your brokenness, in your desolation, Jesus is calling you. Maybe he isn't calling with audible words, but he is present, and he longs to be *with you.*

  Now, I don't know about you, but I can spend so much time calling out to God and waiting for his discernible response that I sometimes miss the fact he is calling to me also. As my spiritual director, Jenni, frequently reminds me, "Just your desire to be with God is God drawing you to himself."

DELAYED PRESENCE

Jesus draws near to us in our pain. Jesus invites us to draw near to him in our pain. The invitation is there. But how do we respond in Jesus' seeming absence? When his manifest presence isn't, well, manifest?

Of all the names Jesus could have ascribed to himself, one of the first names he chose was Immanuel, which means "God with us." Almost eight hundred years before the birth of Jesus, Isaiah prophesied to King Ahaz, "The Lord himself will give you a sign: The virgin will conceive and give birth to a son, and will call him Immanuel" (Isa. 7:14). Presence. God in the flesh. One of us. That is who Jesus is.

Names have power because they convey identity.[10] A placeholder for your person, they declare who you are—your essence—even in your absence.

But what are we supposed to do when Jesus' identity of being *with us* seems at odds with our experience of his absence? What about

- when his dear friend Lazarus died?
- when David died?
- when your dream, belief, family member, relationship, health, or sense of well-being died?

Where is God's promised presence that brings life?

Martha's reaction to Jesus' delayed physical presence gives us some clues of how we can respond to God in our own seasons of death—and how he responds to us. Mary and Martha asked Jesus to come, but he didn't show. And in the busyness surrounding death, life keeps going. Mary and Martha make funeral preparations, prepare Lazarus's body, secure a tomb, and hire and host mourners. Then four days after Lazarus is laid to rest—*after* the funeral!—Jesus shows up:

> When Martha heard that Jesus was coming, she went out to meet him, but Mary stayed at home.

> "Lord," Martha said to Jesus, "if you had been here, my brother would not have died. But I know that even now God will give you whatever you ask."
>
> Jesus said to her, "Your brother will rise again."
>
> Martha answered, "I know he will rise again in the resurrection at the last day."
>
> Jesus said to her, "I am the resurrection and the life. The one who believes in me will live, even though they die; and whoever lives by believing in me will never die. Do you believe this?"
>
> "Yes, Lord," she replied, "I believe that you are the Messiah, the Son of God, who is to come into the world." (John 11:20-27)

Before Jesus can even get to her house, Martha meets him outside (John 11:20). Martha may have been distracted and missed her chance to sit at Jesus' feet (Luke 10:38-42) when he was last with them (haven't we all?), but she isn't going to miss him this time.

And so Martha begins: With fact. With doubt. And with confession. She lays it all at Jesus' feet in the form of a shortened lament—*turn*, *complain*, *ask*, and *trust*: "Lord (*turn*), if you had been here, my brother wouldn't have died (*complaint and implied ask that Lazarus would live*). Yet even now I know that whatever you ask from God, God will give you (*trust*)" (John 11:21-22, CSB).

Even though Jesus is now physically present with Martha, all is not well. Jesus' presence has not resolved Martha's grief. In fact, his delayed presence has compounded her grief. Yet Martha holds firmly to what she knows to be true about God. She professes that God has the power to do anything he desires, and she correctly identifies the relationship between the Father and the Son (John 14:9-11). When Jesus clarifies that Lazarus will live again, Martha—still not fully understanding—articulates her hope in the resurrection (John 11:24).

So Jesus speaks clearly and directly to Martha: "I am the resurrection and the life. The one who believes in me will live, even though they die; and whoever lives by believing in me will never die" (John 11:25-26).

Martha has come to Jesus concerned with the death of her beloved brother and Jesus' delayed presence. But Jesus isn't as concerned with answering her unspoken questions as he is with giving her a more precious gift—the gift of himself.

THE GIFT

If you're someone who loves logic, order, and processes and believes that A should always lead to B, then Jesus' words to Martha may not be very comforting. *Jesus, answer my questions first! Fix my problem now, then I'll be better prepared to receive your presence later.*

But isn't that the confounding and beautifully mysterious way of Jesus? How often do people in the Bible approach Jesus—sometimes not even knowing his identity—with a question or need only to be given something they didn't ask for or even know they needed?

The woman at the well questioned why a Jewish man was asking a Samaritan woman for a drink. Not only did she learn about living water, but the Messiah was revealed to her, and many in her town believed in Jesus because of her testimony (John 4:9, 26, 39).

When a room was too crowded for their group to pass through, friends of a paralyzed man lowered him through the roof. But before the man picked up his mat and walked home, Jesus forgave him of his sins (Luke 5:18-20).

Nathanael asked Jesus how he knew him. Jesus' response not only elicited a profession of faith from Nathanael but also included the promise that Nathanael would be given sight to see "'heaven open, and the angels of God ascending and descending on' the Son of Man" (John 1:48-51).

Crying at the empty tomb, Mary asked the "gardener" to tell her where Jesus' body had been placed. But instead of a location, she was given the risen Lord and heard him speak her name with knowing: *Mary*. Mary was then commissioned to be the first person to proclaim that Jesus had risen (John 20:15-18).

Two disciples walking to Emmaus attempted to explain to a "visitor" their devastation concerning Jesus' failed attempt to redeem Israel. Not only did they receive an exegesis of the messianic Scriptures by Jesus himself, but their eyes were opened to recognize that the triumphant and resurrected Jesus was present with them (Luke 24:19-21, 27, 30-31).

Over and over again, people were given *more* than they asked for (see Eph. 3:20). And the same thing that was true for Martha is true for you and for me. While Jesus did speak to Martha's concerns, he also saw her heart and spoke to her deepest need: her desire to know and be fully known by God (John 11:4, 23, 25-27).

You are fully known, and you do not fully know God. But because of love, he invites you to know him deeper still and experience the fullness of life: "*I am* the resurrection and the life" (John 11:25, emphasis mine).

When you're in a house of mourning, there is no better gift than life. So Jesus brought that real and everlasting life into Martha and Mary's home, in his own person, and later purchased it with his own blood. Jesus drew near and gently reframed Martha's perspective of death by revealing his true identity: resurrection life. *I am what you're seeking! I am life itself!*

In response, Martha professed her faith in Jesus and received a gift that would "never perish, spoil or fade" (1 Pet. 1:4). And all this happened while Lazarus was still *dead*.

In answer to "Will you be with me in *this*?"—in this suffering, in living in a broken world, in facing and fearing loss—God became one of us, and now Love is forevermore wrapped in fragile human flesh (see John 1:14).

I don't believe God causes pain so you will know him better. That's too reductionistic, and quite frankly, hurtful. But I do believe that God wastes nothing. I believe that pain and suffering, while certainly unwelcome, can be an opportunity for you to become undone. And in the undoing, for God to meet you in your deepest places of hurt and provide the hope and healing you didn't even know you needed.

REFLECTION EXERCISE

In place of answering questions, go to tiffanystein.com for a guided exercise through John 11:25-26. My prayer is that instead of just learning more *about* God you'll spend intentional time *with* God by meditating on his Word.

PRAYER

God, thank you for always being present and for speaking through your Son, the Holy Spirit, and the Bible. I'd love to experience your manifest presence more often, especially when I'm undone by my pain and grief, but I also know that your silence is just for a season. Would you remind me that you're with me in my suffering? Would you show me life once more? Amen.

Even though I walk
    through the darkest valley,
I will fear no evil,
    for *you are with me*;
your rod and your staff,
    they comfort me.

PSALM 23:4, EMPHASIS MINE

Interlude

The Spirit of God has made me;
the breath of the Almighty gives me life.

JOB 33:4

Let's go back into that counseling room with God. You're exhausted from the upheaval of words, thoughts, and emotions. You've said your piece, cried your tears, ranted, railed, wrestled with God himself, sat in the dark, dared to hope in the silence, and now it's all out there. *It* sits between you and God: a mountain of fragments that once formed your life. You are undone in both your grief and your longing, and there is nothing left to do but draw a breath and pause.

There is silence. And then he says,

May I?

I've heard your accusations, questions, fears, doubts, and concerns. I feel your anger toward me and see the pain both my presence and my perceived absence have caused you.

You may feel that I'm not the God you thought you knew, and perhaps that's a good thing. But I do know you, beloved. So may

I sift through the pieces with you? Would you allow me to discard what is untrue of me? Of you? Would you allow me to add new pieces? Pieces that better reflect the true me? The true you?

I promise that I won't leave you undone. I always finish what I start (Phil. 1:6). And since we're starting something new together, let's begin at the beginning.

He crosses through the fragments and sits down next to you. Love has spoken. And again there is silence (see 1 Kings 19:12).

* * *

If you're able, I want you to imagine Jesus sitting next to you in a companionable quiet. It's not the silence of absence nor the white noise of distraction but the kind of quiet that comes after a storm has raged. After you've smashed all your kitchen glasses or sobbed on your bedroom floor or spent hours pouring out your pain to a friend, there comes a gentle lull. A momentary pause insignificant to anyone but you. But you feel it. Something has shifted in your heart and mind. God has come near. And for this moment, at least, you are content to simply be in his presence. To be known. To be loved. And to experience the miraculous yet mundane act of breathing in and breathing out. For where there is breath, there is life.

Sit in this moment as long as you would like. You don't need to say, pray, think, or do anything. Simply be present.

THE THRESHOLD

That day when evening came, he said to his disciples, "Let us go over to the other side." Leaving the crowd behind,

> they took him along, just as he was, in the boat. There were also other boats with him. A furious squall came up, and the waves broke over the boat, so that it was nearly swamped. Jesus was in the stern, sleeping on a cushion. The disciples woke him and said to him, "Teacher, don't you care if we drown?"
>
> He got up, rebuked the wind and said to the waves, "Quiet! Be still!" Then the wind died down and it was completely calm.
>
> He said to his disciples, "Why are you so afraid? Do you still have no faith?"
>
> They were terrified and asked each other, "Who is this? Even the wind and the waves obey him!" (Mark 4:35-41)

We are at a threshold between disillusionment and sight. The Mark 4 passage sums up our journey so far:

- Like the disciples, you thought you knew Jesus. He was with you, and you were doing life together, maybe even ministering together. Then the storms of life came, you were near drowning, and Jesus was caught sleeping. Sleeping through a crisis comes across as uncaring, distant, and removed at best. But to be asleep while with you in the capsizing boat? That's just cruel. *Don't you care, God?*

- Yet God does care. Jesus has come near. To the chaos of death represented by the raging sea, Jesus commands, "Quiet! Be still!" (Mark 4:39).

- Here is the God who calms the storm after sleeping and raises the dead after delaying. *Who is he?*

It's natural to be disillusioned with or disappointed in someone or something when you discover them to be less than expected. But the righting of disillusionment isn't fulfilled expectations, as wonderful as that would be. It's clarity to see things rightly, as they are. Because what if your expectations are wrong? What if the someone you're disappointed in isn't *less than* expected but *more than* expected?

> My heart is not proud, Lord,
> my eyes are not haughty;
> I do not concern myself with great matters
> or things too wonderful for me.
> But I have calmed and quieted myself,
> I am like a weaned child with its mother;
> like a weaned child I am content.
>
> Israel, put your hope in the Lord
> both now and forevermore. (Ps. 131:1-3)

Psalm 131 speaks to where we are going. And it is to sitting in this mystery of *more than* that we now turn.

You see, the threshold is an invitation to reflect on where you've been as you prepare for what's ahead. It's a place to metabolize change, practice gratitude, and present your requests before God. It's also a place to celebrate your progress as you sit in the tension of having come this far already but not yet being where you long to be. (Oh, sanctification! Why must you take a lifetime?)

REFLECTION QUESTIONS

1. As you look back on your journey thus far, what has most encouraged or helped you?

2. What has surprised you about the journey, God, or yourself?

3. Are there any untruths you've uncovered thus far about God or yourself that you'd like to lay down? What truths would you like to replace those distorted images with?

4. As your journey increasingly takes you toward reorientation and new life, what are some of your desires and fears? In one sentence, what is it that you most desire from God?

5. How can a trusted person best accompany you moving forward?

If you invited a trusted friend or family member back in chapter 4 to encourage you along the way, take a moment to text, email, or call that person. Thank them for their support, prayers, and presence in your journey thus far. Update them on where you've been and how you feel regarding hope. If something specific is on your mind or heart, share it with them and invite them to join you in praying about it. If you don't yet have a trusted person, now is a great time to invite someone to join you and catch them up on where you've been.

PART 3

light

8

Suffering Love: *Joy and Sorrow*

Weeping may tarry for the night,
but joy comes with the morning.

PSALM 30:5, ESV

And love is always sacrificial—partly because anything we love we will lose in this life. There is no love of others that does not necessarily open us to loss, wound, and grief. But we do not grieve without hope.

DOUGLAS McKELVEY, *EVERY MOMENT HOLY II*

It is Lent 2024, and once again I'm living in the ICU. It is a familiar trauma.

His lungs are failing, so he is rapidly intubated. The ventilator breathes on his behalf, robbing him of the ability to speak. I've only just arrived, and there is panic in his eyes. He believes he is choking and looks to me for help.

The alarms signal danger: His pulse is too low, and he is in danger of cardiac arrest. Nurses rush in, and I run out. This cross is too heavy to bear. I've lived this before.

It is midnight in the hospital parking lot, and I'm sitting alone in my parked car. As I pound the steering wheel, I sob and scream at God, "No, God. No! This can't be happening again. Please don't let him die."

But I am needed. This is what I came here to do: to accompany the suffering, provide comfort and assistance where I can (2 Cor. 1:4), be present in the face of death, and if necessary, also say goodbye. And so I walk back into the hospital. This is the power of Christ in me (Eph. 3:20).

He cannot advocate for himself, so we, the family, encircle his bed and advocate for him. We do not leave his side. We diligently research his rare condition, follow the peaks and valleys of the monitors, meet with specialists, take detailed notes, interrogate the doctors, request more pain medicine, are grateful for the sedatives that grant him peaceful sleep, and pray for a miracle.

And oh, how I urgently pray for a miracle. How I pray that the treatments will be effective and that new life will course through his body. How I pray for the peace that surpasses all understanding (Phil. 4:7) and that the God of comfort will be near (2 Cor. 1:3).

I have the night shifts. I diligently watch and wait.

But I've been here before, and I know the warning signs. I see the shift when his left lung collapses. A few days later the treatment has proved to be ineffective. All medical options are exhausted. This is the end.

And once again I find myself draped across a therapy dog, wetting its fur with my tears and clinging to it like hope is only found in the embrace of a dog. Dusty is a white standard poodle with tight curls. Six years ago, in the NICU, it was a large, shaggy goldendoodle named Badger. In the midst of impending death, warm, chocolate eyes look deep into my soul. And I can see love there.

Once more it is Saturday night, and we are waiting. Watching. Praying. Will there be a miracle?

His breathing slows, then ceases. The doctor declares the time of death, and it is finished. Grieving family members leave the hospital laden with belongings but not with their beloved.

I stare at his worn wristband, eerily like the one I have at home. Mine reads, "David Allen Stein." This one reads, "Mark Allen Stein." We named David in honor of his grandfather, and I prayed that David would grow to be a man of God like his father and his father before him. But now my father-in-law is gone too.

It is Holy Saturday, and tomorrow is Easter. I'm grateful that Jesus is no longer dead in a tomb. He is alive. But tomorrow we won't be celebrating. We are grieving. And we will be grieving for a while.

Lord, have mercy.

As a father has compassion on his children,
　　so the LORD has compassion on those who fear him;
for he knows how we are formed,
　　he remembers that we are dust. (Ps. 103:13–14)

APRIL 2024

In the middle of writing this book, I got *the* call—the life-defining "Hello?" that forever separates the *before* from the *after*. My larger-than-life and perfectly healthy father-in-law, Mark, was at the emergency room. And almost six years to the day after David's death, Mark died. It was Holy Saturday.

On Easter Sunday, we spent the day planning Mark's funeral, writing his obituary, and selecting photos for the slideshow. I was gutted and had self-medicated with copious amounts of chips and salsa.

As Jason and I were crawling into bed, a fresh wave of grief pummeled me again. Huge, giant sobs shook my body. Jason hugged me until the crying subsided. And then, with wet tears still drying on my face, Jason turned and jokingly asked, "Well, do you think you can get a few chapters out of this?"

And suddenly we were both snort-laughing because all this was ridiculous. Losing David was enough to meditate on for a lifetime. And yet here I am writing the second half of this book in real time as God and I process *yet another* traumatic loss.

God, don't waste the pain.

It's a vulnerable and humbling place to be. My emotions are raw and real, and the wounds are tender to the touch. Everything in me wants to skip over the loss of Mark and only tell you about the loss of David, a loss that is now more "manageable" and less painful since time has passed.

But that's not the promise I made to you. I promised to be a companion on your journey. And if we truly walk this road of grief together, then I need to continue inviting you into my real life, just as you've allowed me the honor of accompanying you in this season of your real life.

What I thought was merely a journey from grief to hope

continues to be much more. And now I see it for what it is—a pilgrimage. A sacred journey "into the heart and life of God."[1]

And in this particular phase of the journey, I find myself dwelling in the strange land of joyful sorrow, where laughter can somehow follow tears on Easter.

* * *

"Don't worry. This funeral won't be a sad one," the pastor confidently declared to our family. "The days for crying have passed. Mark's service is going to be one of laughing and celebrating!"

Two days later, my sister-in-law, Megan, pulled me aside and whispered, "I'm still crying. Is something wrong with me?" Her father hadn't even been buried yet! But somehow she was supposed to be done with lamenting and have moved on to rejoicing.

If you've ever attended the funeral of a believer: Can we all just admit that the service is often awkward? *Cringey* is how I'd describe sitting with strangers for an intense hour of emotional gymnastics as the officiant struggles to hit the right tone. Sometimes the officiant veers off into grievous lament without hope, leaving everyone wrecked, and other times he or she preaches glib hope without acknowledging the weighty sorrow that undergirds true hope. Both extremes are dangerous.

But you know it when the officiant finds that sacred middle ground, somehow blending sorrow with joy and joy with sorrow in a way that feels natural, genuine, and true to the human experience. There are tears. There is laughter. And there is love.

I posted on Facebook on David's fifth anniversary:

> The misconception about grief is that it's something you can heal from. But grief isn't an illness. There's not

> something wrong with you that needs to be fixed. Grief is love enduring. And as long as there is love, there will always be some measure of grief.
>
> In the five years since I kissed my baby boy goodbye, I've learned powerful lessons about love. I've learned that love can grow and flourish even without it being reciprocated, that love transcends the grave, that love is the unbreaking tether that binds us together now and for all eternity, and that to love is to experience both joy and sorrow simultaneously, overflowing and poured out.[2]

Six years later, I'm still crying. *And* I've experienced profound joy.

I realize that your tragic loss may not be the loss of a loved one or that you may not know if you'll see your loved one in heaven. (I'm truly sorry.) But whatever your loss, there comes a point in your journey when you realize that life rarely hands you pure happily-ever-after endings. Instead you get joy and sorrow—rejoicing and mourning—all shaken up like a fizzing bottle of Coke spilling stickily into your cupped hands.

And oh, friend, if you're despairing, how I long to promise you that your pain will gradually diminish, what you've lost will be restored, and your future is even brighter than you imagined. But unfortunately, you and I still live in a sin-saturated world, where pain remains, no matter how much healing we experience. And if what you are waiting for as you heal and grow after loss is the complete absence of pain, you will remain disappointed in God and disgruntled for the rest of your life.

Or perhaps you expected the pain to linger but felt guilty and confused when joy flickered and then took up permanent residence in the midst of your profound pain. *Is it okay to experience joy while mourning? Is it okay to smile and not feel sad all the time?*

More to the point: What has joy to do with sorrow?

BRIGHT SADNESS

To be honest, most of us don't know how to inhabit the in-between space of holding two seemingly opposing emotions. Many of us have been taught that joy and sorrow are on the same continuum and that the goal (ahem—the *godly* goal) is to move further to the right.

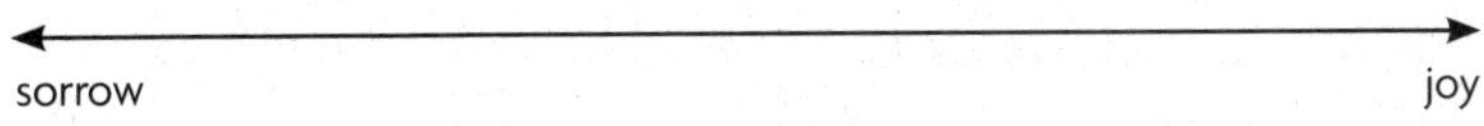

It wasn't until I went to grief counseling that I learned that sorrow and joy are actually two overlapping, coexisting realities.

We live in this world with all its sorrow, yet it's not our final home (John 15:19; Phil. 3:20). We rejoice that Jesus defeated death (2 Tim. 1:10) while also mourning that death has not yet been put away once and for all (Rev. 20:14). So we neither deny nor glorify the sorrow but instead grant ourselves permission to feel, carry, and sometimes experience a multitude of emotions all at the same time.

To carry joy and sorrow simultaneously is to know a "bright sadness," a term used by the Eastern Orthodox Church to describe the Lenten season. Yet the term could be attributed to many seasons of life, including the shift from disorientation to reorientation.

The Rev. Dr. Andrew Grosso writes that in the Eastern tradition "the Greek word *charmolypê* . . . can be variously translated as 'bright sadness,' 'joyful mourning,' or 'bitter sweetness.' Part of what this term is intended to express is the way joy and sorrow inform one another in the life of faith. . . . The correlation between them is positive, not negative: we're able to enter more fully into one by learning to enter more fully into the other."[3]

To proclaim that experiencing sorrow can lead to greater joy and intimacy with God might seem like a stretch, so let's consider Job, a wealthy man who lived in the ancient Near East around the time of Abraham. He "was blameless and upright; he feared God and shunned evil" (Job 1:1).

Yet Job lost

- all his oxen, donkeys, sheep, and camels;
- all the servants caring for his animals, who were brutally slaughtered with swords or devoured by fire; and
- all ten of his children, who were killed in a freak roof collapse (Job 1:13-19).

In one day, through no fault of his own, Job lost his livelihood, laborers, and legacy. Then the next day Satan afflicted Job with "painful sores from the soles of his feet to the crown of his head" (Job 2:7). Instead of offering solace, Job's angry wife encouraged him to "curse God and die" (Job 2:9) while his friends vainly theorized as to what he had done to deserve such suffering. It seems that Job's only comfort in this entire ordeal was the piece of broken pottery he used to scratch his oozing boils (Job 2:8).

Modern sermons make much of Job, and rightly so, because after experiencing these losses,

> he fell to the ground in worship and said:
>
> "Naked I came from my mother's womb,
> and naked I will depart.
> The Lord gave and the Lord has taken away;
> may the name of the Lord be praised." (Job 1:20-21)

But the story doesn't end there. Job was human, after all. After he worshiped, Job struggled to comprehend God's sovereignty and wrestled with "the paradox of seemingly unjust suffering"[4] (Job 3–37).

God eventually replied to Job, but he didn't address Job's questions. Instead he asked Job a series of questions that broadened Job's perspective and helped him realize that God's purposes and plans were much more than he could comprehend (Job 38:2; 42:3). Job's response was one of contrition and evidence of a deepening relationship with God: "My ears had heard of you but now my eyes have *seen you*" (Job 42:5, emphasis mine).

God also restored Job's health and fortune by giving him twice as much as he had before in addition to blessing him with ten more children (Job 42:10, 13). But you know what Job didn't get back? His first ten children!

Job's dead children didn't come back to life, and nothing—not even the joy of welcoming additional children—could undo the pain. Job received God's blessing (joy), *and* he still grieved the traumatic loss of his children (sorrow). The apostle James writes, "As you know, we count as blessed those who have persevered. You have heard of

Job's perseverance and have seen what the Lord finally brought about. The Lord is full of compassion and mercy" (James 5:11).

At first glance, James appears to be commending Job for persevering through suffering while awaiting God's response and subsequent healing and restoration (Job 38–42). But might James also be praising Job for the way he persevered through the tension of joy and sorrow for the rest of his life? For the way Job celebrated ten birthdays and mourned an anniversary every year thereafter for 140 long years? For the ways Job loved those in his care while continuing to honor those who were gone? Don't you think the experience of daily entrusting himself to God's mysterious and sometimes bewildering provision would transform Job?

I do. And often that mysterious provision comes in the form of life-giving community where God's mercy and compassion are physically displayed.

HOLDING SPACE

It was a few weeks after David's death, and our worship pastor, Jason Elwell, was checking on me. I expressed to him how painful attending church services was and that many times I had just sat in the shadows of the sanctuary's back row, weeping through the worship songs and corporate prayer time.

With kindness in his eyes and the empathy of one who's been there before, Jason simply said, "Tiffany, we will sing when you cannot sing. We will pray when you cannot pray. We will worship when you cannot worship. We will carry you." In other words, "We, the body of Christ, will stand in for you. We will carry you to the throne room and place you in the arms of Jesus."

If holding space for your own joy and sorrow seems like a daunting task, or if you're thinking, *There's no way I could ever be like Job and celebrate again after all those losses!*, I get you. But that day with my pastor I learned something Job discovered as well. There was space in this place for both my sorrow and my joy and for everyone else's as well. All because of love. All because of community.

Of course, at first, Job's community was lacking. The only figures mentioned prior to Job's restoration are his angry wife and three misguided friends. Job's well-meaning friends traveled to his home to sympathize and empathize with him, where they wept aloud, joined him in lament, and even sat in silence for seven days and nights "because they saw how great his suffering was" (Job 2:11-13).

But once Job opened his mouth and began honestly wrestling with God, they couldn't resist the opportunity to correct his theology. (How helpful!) Where we might expect comfort, encouragement, and a reminder to consider the past faithfulness of God, Job's friends instead basically sent him articles, podcasts, and sermons about the dangers of hidden sin, the just wrath of God, and a five-step plan for ensuring genuine repentance. In other words: *Job, you must've really sinned big to deserve such punishment. God is really angry with you. What did you do?*

It's easy to criticize Job's friends for their self-righteousness and distorted understanding of God, but haven't we all been there, seeking to help when all we're doing is unintentionally causing hurt? I know I have. *Lord, forgive us.*

So God points us to a better way.

Ever the God who invites truth and true intimacy, God confronted Job's three friends:

> After the Lord had said these things to Job, he said to Eliphaz the Temanite, "I am angry with you and your two friends, because you have not spoken the truth about me, as my

> servant Job has. So now take seven bulls and seven rams and go to my servant Job and sacrifice a burnt offering for yourselves. My servant Job will pray for you, and I will accept his prayer and not deal with you according to your folly." (Job 42:7-8)

Where there was distortion about God's character (folly), God granted sight (truth). And because God is both just and merciful, he accepted burnt offerings and Job's prayers on behalf of his friends instead of giving them what they deserved. In God's great plan of redemption and restoration, Job, the one who lacked faithful friends, ended up being a faithful friend by forgiving his unjust accusers and humbly interceding on their behalf.

Now notice what comes next: "All his brothers and sisters and everyone who had known him before came and ate with him in his house. They comforted and consoled him over all the trouble the LORD had brought on him, and each one gave him a piece of silver and a gold ring" (Job 42:11). Don't miss the significance of this verse. The critical element to Job being able to abide in the tension of joy and sorrow for the rest of his life was being surrounded with life-giving community! This kind of community can look like sharing a meal together, giving and receiving genuine comfort and consolation, being physically present, and giving material possessions to provide for the needs of others. It can also look like being quick to forgive when you've been wronged (because hurt people sometimes hurt people) and praying for God's healing work in the lives of others. It's the simple and everyday acts of showing up and pointing to God in word and deed.

Friend, godly community is what will allow you to abide in the lifelong tension of joy and sorrow as well. Your community will be a placeholder for you and can help you pace accordingly. When you cannot see and your perspective is clouded, your community can remind you of what was, what is, and what is yet to be. They can speak truth to you, pray for you, fast and mourn with you, and feast and rejoice with you. They can be a physical expression of God's love for you.

John, the beloved disciple, says in 1 John 4:12, "No one has ever seen God; but if we love one another, God lives in us and his love is made complete in us."

God's intention has always been that love would be made real in Christian community. What might that practically look like?

If you're trying to hold space for a loved one's joy and sorrow as you accompany them through grief, here are a few suggestions:

- Be present. Just show up. (But perhaps call or text first.)

- Remember that your physical presence matters. Even sitting in the same room with someone can convey solidarity. As appropriate, offer hugs or hold their hand.

- Be slow to speak. Theorizing, offering platitudes, giving unwanted advice, issuing "I-told-you-so" statements, passing along a five-step plan to happiness, and exclaiming "I know exactly what you're going through!" before launching into your own lengthy story are rarely helpful. (Diatribes on the current state of world affairs should also be avoided.)

- Check in after everyone else has moved on. While your world goes on after your friend's divorce, surgery, family funeral, diagnosis, or other tragic event, their life is forever changed. They still need you and want to know that they haven't been forgotten.

- Help meet tangible needs: Mow the lawn. Email a gift card. Babysit the kids. Drop off a meal. Pick up their medicine or groceries. Walk the dog. (Offering to do something specific is more helpful than asking an overwhelmed person what they need; they may not know.)
- Recognize that you may feel uncomfortable in this in-between space. That's okay. Your friend is probably uncomfortable as well. Push through.
- Share a meal together with no expectations. Laughing and crying are optional.
- Acknowledge the sorrow that still lingers. Don't deny or minimize their pain.
- Acknowledge the joy, even if the arrival of joy in their life seems too early or too much to you.
- Contribute beauty to their home with a living plant, colorful card, framed art print, photo of you two together, meaningful souvenir, or another gift. A visible reminder of beauty can refresh their perspective and spark joy.
- Make space to delight in the little things with them. Take them to lunch at a new restaurant. Go for a walk together and count how many different types of flowers you see. Take a photo of something that inspires you and send it to them.
- Text them something amusing or funny. As insignificant as it seems, sending a comical meme lets the other person know you're thinking of them and deepens your connection.

- Share a favorite song. Sending a video of yourself dancing to it is highly recommended.
- Start a shared gratitude list on a note-taking app. You'll be amazed by how gratitude cultivates joy.
- If a birthday, anniversary, or other significant date is approaching, ask how they'd like to mark the occasion. Offer to accompany them and/or plan the day for them.

If you're the person living in the tension of joy and sorrow, which of these practices could you invite others into? In my experience, people usually want to help but don't know where to start. It's okay to lovingly ask for what you need or desire from the safe and trusted people in your life.

And if you're in a season like Job was, where your community is lacking, unhelpful, hurtful, or nonexistent, I lament with you. That is not the way it's supposed to be! You were created for community.

Proverbs 18:24 reads, "One who has unreliable friends soon comes to ruin, but there is a friend who sticks closer than a brother." The *only* reliable friend who will *never* fail you, abandon you, or betray you is the one who is your true brother, Jesus (Heb. 2:11). And in God's goodness and great mystery, we are invited to participate in the perfect and complete community of the triune God. He who lacks nothing and needs nothing beckons you and me to find in him the fulfilling relationship we all desire and to live as those who are truly loved.

I join with you in praying that God will provide you with faithful, loving friends and that, most importantly, you will find refuge in the fellowship of God. For it is right here—in the joys and sorrows of life—that you are being formed into a person of hope who reflects the cruciform love of Christ.

REFLECTION QUESTIONS

1. How have you experienced the intermingling of joy and sorrow? Have you welcomed it, felt distressed by it, or been surprised by it?

2. Where have you seen God's provision of compassion and mercy (James 5:11) in your own life?

3. Do you feel that you have life-giving community surrounding and supporting you? If so, which of these practices will you invite others into?

PRAYER

*God, I don't thank you for the sorrows of life, but I thank you for the beauty you are fashioning from them. Do your work in me and cultivate joy within my heart. Please grant me life-giving community, and may I be a faithful friend who is quick to hold space for others. Amen.***

May the grace of the Lord Jesus Christ, and the love of God, and the fellowship of the Holy Spirit be with you all.

2 CORINTHIANS 13:14

** For a longer prayer you can pray in community, go to tiffanystein.com.

9

Dare to Delight: *Celebration*

The LORD takes pleasure in his people;
he adorns the humble with salvation.
Let the faithful celebrate in triumphal glory;
let them shout for joy on their beds.

PSALM 149:4-5, CSB

It was just before Easter. Mark was still in critical condition, we were grieving the loss of a dear friend who had died in a car accident just days before, and David's anniversary was only a few weeks away. This was a season of sorrow.

And yet the resurrection of Jesus proves that life triumphs over death and proclaims that life is to be celebrated. So perhaps I shouldn't be surprised that I found celebratory joy in the most unlikely place: the hospital gift shop.

I'm not a dress person, but the long and flowy white concoction in the gift shop's display window caught my eye. I passed by the dress-wearing mannequin dozens of times a day as I went to and from the ICU, carrying meals, snacks, and water bottles for family members; running errands; taking phone calls; prayer walking; and giving family members precious alone time with Mark.

With each hurried step and passing glance, the dress beckoned me. In an austere environment devoted to holding off death, here was a garment celebrating the hope and beauty of new life (see Rom. 8:11). *I'm fully cleansed of my sins! I've been washed "whiter than snow" (Ps. 51:7)! All things are being made new thanks to Jesus' resurrection (Isa. 65:17)!*

I began to dream of Mark being stable enough for me to go home for a few days to celebrate Easter with my family at our new church. I anticipated trading the stress and urgency of the hospital for children giggling as they hunted for plastic eggs in our backyard, friends lingering around our dinner table, and an Easter spent rejoicing in Jesus' defeat of death.

Early one morning while on a coffee run, I finally ducked in to try on the dress. Looking in the mirror at the exhausted woman clothed in bright, billowy fabric, I felt ridiculous. A new dress wasn't going to fool anyone.

But maybe it wasn't about fooling anyone. Perhaps it was about a declaration. A declaration that, in the midst of the pain and the mundane, here was something good and praiseworthy. So I dared to celebrate and left the gift shop with an oversized hot-pink shopping bag. Because some years you coordinate Easter outfits for the entire family. Other years you buy an Easter dress from the hospital gift shop. And both are good.

DELIGHTING IN GOD

When you think of celebrating, what comes to mind? Do you imagine festive parties with balloons, buttercream-frosted cake, and themed photo props? Line dancing at a wedding? Going on an extended family vacation? Or perhaps you think of something more intimate and less boisterous, like receiving a card of congratulations from a dear friend? Enjoying a celebratory glass of your favorite beverage with a few people in the comfort of your own home? Reading a corporate memo announcing your promotion?

The beauty of celebration is that it need not be expensive, loud, deliberate, or formal—although it can be—because celebration isn't so much a single action as it is a way of being. Dallas Willard writes, "We engage in celebration when we enjoy ourselves, our life, our world, *in conjunction with* our faith and confidence in God's greatness, beauty, and goodness."[1] In other words, our ability to experience delight and joy is grounded in the praiseworthy, unchanging character of God as opposed to our ever-changing circumstances.

So whether the season we're in is painful or relatively pain free, we can celebrate because we worship the God who celebrates. I don't know if that fact astounds you, but it astounds me. God celebrates! He delights. He rejoices. He sings. God isn't a stoic, reserved, distant god but the God who is moved by love.

This is how one scholar defines God's joy: "God rejoices in the well-being and faithfulness of his covenant people, and in the repentance and conversion of sinners. He brings joy to his people, who rejoice in his presence and faithfulness."[2]

To better understand the biblical concept of celebration, we need to pay close attention to related words like *joy*, *gratitude*, *thanksgiving*, *rejoice*, *worship*, and *praise*. In just a brief sampling of verses related to God's joy, here's what we learn:

- *God is the source of joy.* "I have told you this so that my *joy* may be in you and that your *joy* may be complete" (John 15:11, emphasis mine).

- *There is rejoicing in heaven when a sinner repents.* "What man among you, who has a hundred sheep and loses one of them, does not leave the ninety-nine in the open field and go after the lost one until he finds it? When he has found it, he *joyfully* puts it on his shoulders, and coming home, he calls his friends and neighbors together, saying to them, '*Rejoice* with me, because I have found my lost sheep!' I tell you, in the same way, there will be more *joy* in heaven over one sinner who repents than over ninety-nine righteous people who don't need repentance" (Luke 15:4-7, CSB, emphasis mine).

- *God celebrates when someone places their faith in him.* "The father said to his servants, 'Quick! Bring the best robe and put it on him. Put a ring on his finger and sandals on his feet. Bring the fattened calf and kill it. Let's have a feast and *celebrate.* For this son of mine was dead and is alive again; he was lost and is found.' So they began to *celebrate*" (Luke 15:22-24, emphasis mine).

- *God delights in his chosen people.* "The LORD your God is in your midst, a mighty one who will save; he will *rejoice* over you with gladness; he will quiet you by his love; he will *exult* over you with loud singing" (Zeph. 3:17, ESV, emphasis mine).

And since God himself is the joy giver and originator of celebration, it makes sense that he invites us, his image bearers, to join in that celebration. Of course, joy isn't something you create or produce on your own. You aren't fighting the forces of darkness by yourself. The Holy Spirit empowers you, and joy itself is a fruit of the Holy Spirit and a good gift of God (Gal. 5:22).

God, the source of joy and the one who delights in you, gifts you joy and opportunities to exhibit it. Then, in response to God's greatness and goodness, you're invited to rejoice in him, which deepens your enjoyment of him. In so doing, celebration becomes "the completion of worship."[3]

CELEBRATION: THE COMPLETION OF WORSHIP

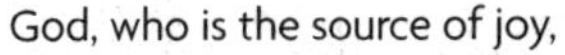

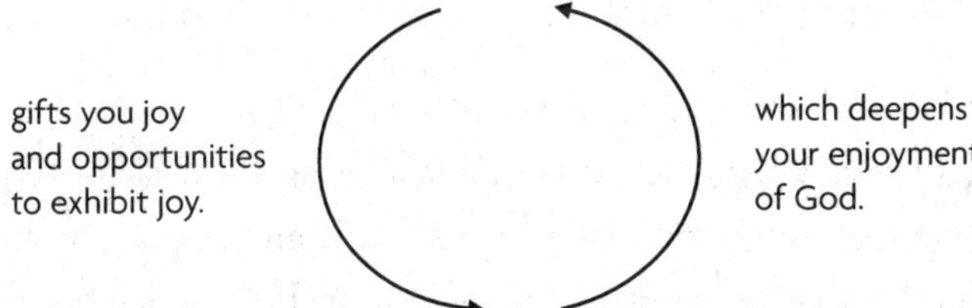

You respond to God's greatness
and goodness by rejoicing in Him,

A REASON TO CELEBRATE

Admittedly, celebrating when things are going well is easy. But to dare to celebrate and delight in God when things are not as they should be? Now, that's revolutionary!

Karina Kreminski concurs: "Joy is subversive in that it proclaims laughter, contentment and hope in the midst of a reality which seeks to convince us this is all there is and we should hope for nothing more. Joy overturns and challenges this despairing thought."[4]

And that's the wonder of joy and celebration: When life has already been turned upside down and inside out, practicing subversive joy can help turn things right again. Because celebration doesn't require life to be perfect or our circumstances to be good. Rather, celebration intentionally invites life and goodness into even our darkest moments—a divine interruption of sorts. It is about this practice of poking holes in the darkness that Richard Foster observes,

> *God's desire is to transform the misery, not bypass it.*
>
> We need to understand that God does at times give us an infusion of joy even in our bitterness and hard-heartedness. But that is the abnormal situation. *God's normal means of bringing his joy is by redeeming and sanctifying the ordinary junctures of human life.*[5]

And friend, what could be more normal to the human experience than life and death?

Just as each of our individual stories has a beginning, middle, and end, so, too, does the story of Lazarus. And everyone thought Lazarus's death was the end of his story (John 11:21, 32, 37).

But where we see an ending, Jesus sees a new beginning.

Remember, Jesus came to Bethany after Lazarus had been dead for four days. He met Martha outside and revealed himself to be the resurrection and the life. Then he called for Mary (John 11:25, 28).

> When Mary reached the place where Jesus was and saw him, she fell at his feet and said, "Lord, if you had been here, my brother would not have died."
>
> When Jesus saw her weeping, and the Jews who had come along with her also weeping, he was deeply moved in spirit and troubled. "Where have you laid him?" he asked.
>
> "Come and see, Lord," they replied.
>
> Jesus wept. (John 11:32-35)

Interestingly, both sisters repeated the same refrain: "Lord, if you had been here, my brother would not have died." So Jesus asked each sister a personal question inviting increased trust in him in response to his self-revelation. He asked Martha, "Do you believe this?" (John 11:26). And he inquired of Mary, "Where have you laid him?" (John 11:34).

Notice that Jesus didn't ask where Lazarus was with the unconcern of someone typing an address into Google Maps or the uncertainty of someone asking for directions after driving around lost at night. Jesus instead asked the question with power, indignation, and intensity: "Where have you laid him?"

Biblical scholar Andreas J. Köstenberger writes, "'Deeply moved' (TNIV) hardly does justice to the underlying Greek word ἐμβριμάομαι (*embrimaomai*), which has the connotation of snorting (in animals). Thus, Jesus is shown here not so much to express empathy or grief as to bristle at his imminent encounter with and assault on death."[6]

Recall that in Exodus 34:6 God identifies himself as being "slow to anger," which literally means having "longness of nose."[7] If you think of someone who is easily provoked, their nose may turn red and nostrils flare when they are angry. However, this concrete Hebrew idiom depicts God as being long of nose, or long-suffering. In other words, God's nose doesn't immediately burn hot when he encounters obstruction. His default bent is toward compassion, grace, and patience.

But idiomatically speaking, what did immediately cause Jesus to snort with fury and indignation? Death! Jesus' righteous anger is aroused by death and its claim on his world (Heb. 2:14-15). And Jesus won't stop with just visible agitation or empty rhetoric. He acts on our behalf.

So in anticipation of bringing life to a dead man and rejoicing to a family in mourning, Jesus asked Mary where Lazarus was.

And in anticipation of bringing life to the hurt and broken places in your own life, Jesus asks you the same questions: *Where is the source of your sorrow? Where is death lurking in your life? Show me, beloved, where the pain resides. I want to redeem your suffering. I want you to experience abundant life in me.*

Because where you see the traumatic effects of generational sin, Jesus sees a new generational legacy of faithfulness being planted in you. Where you see fruitless, tiresome work, Jesus sees an ample harvest about to take place. Where you see a diseased mind, Jesus sees wholeness. Where you see rejection, Jesus sees reconciliation.

Jesus doesn't ask where your pain resides because he doesn't know; he knows *exactly* what and where it is (Ps. 56:8). No, Jesus asks because he desires your participation in his healing work of redeeming and restoring (see John 15:5).

Can Jesus heal on his own without your involvement, participation, or even awareness? Absolutely. But there is a special gift for those who courageously respond as Mary and Martha did: "Come and see, Lord" (John 11:34). For when you invite Jesus into your pain and then dare to hope in his goodness, you are better positioned to see God's glory and be an eyewitness of his majesty (see 2 Pet. 1:16)—the true reason for celebration. After all, only those who followed Jesus to the tomb witnessed Jesus raise Lazarus. Jesus beckons, *Come and* truly *see! Come find in me celebratory joy.* And so we see that participating with Jesus in our healing further awakens our awareness of him, which helps us move toward joy, even in the midst of deep sorrow.

> Jesus, once more deeply moved, came to the tomb. It was a cave with a stone laid across the entrance. "Take away the stone," he said.

> "But, Lord," said Martha, the sister of the dead man, "by this time there is a bad odor, for he has been there four days."
>
> Then Jesus said, "Did I not tell you that if you believe, you will see the glory of God?"
>
> So they took away the stone. Then Jesus looked up and said, "Father, I thank you that you have heard me. I knew that you always hear me, but I said this for the benefit of the people standing here, that they may believe that you sent me." (John 11:38-42)

Ever practical, Martha pointed out the inevitable stench of death they would encounter if the stone was rolled away from the tomb. In contrast to their Egyptian neighbors, first-century Jewish people didn't embalm their dead. They merely washed a dead person's body and wrapped it in linen cloth, sometimes with aromatic spices in the windings.[8] And because decomposition of bodies begins immediately, deceased people were often buried the same day they died.

In the recounting of this story, it's as if John wants to make sure his readers understand that Lazarus was *dead* dead. He wasn't freshly dead. He was decaying, rotting-flesh dead.

There are so many things in this life that we aren't prepared to part with: our health, dreams, loved ones, peace, financial stability, jobs, relationships, homes, communities, understanding of self, understanding of God—and the list could go on and on. And what makes the grief even more profoundly devastating is that dead things stay dead. There's no coming back.

But even if dead things could come back to life, no one would want to see their loved ones in a gruesome state of decomposition. Think about it: Never once in movies do people celebrate when they see the "walking dead." Zombies and mummies are horrific because personal experience has taught us that the consequences of death can't be reversed.

But to Martha's objection, Jesus simply ordered, "Take away the stone." I always imagined that Jesus immediately commanded Lazarus to come out after the stone was rolled away, but he didn't. There was an interval in which Jesus affirmed his relationship to the Father and his authority as the Son of God. And as he was speaking to the crowd, the stench of death would have wafted out of the tomb and assaulted everyone's olfactory senses. I suspect some might have turned away, eyes watering, or pulled their tunics over their noses, hoping for a fresh wind to blow away the gag-inducing odor. But then "Jesus called in a loud voice, 'Lazarus, come out!'" (John 11:43). Just in case Mary and Martha's grief, the tomb being sealed for four days, and the stench weren't enough to make the crowd realize that Lazarus had been truly, physically dead, John emphasizes, "The *dead man* came out, his *hands and feet wrapped with strips of linen*, and a *cloth around his face*. Jesus said to them, 'Take off the *grave clothes* and let him go'" (John 11:44, emphasis mine).

Lazarus rising from the dead is the power of God on display. It's the promise of God being fulfilled in the lives of this family (see John 11:22, 40). But most importantly, Lazarus rising from the dead foreshadowed the death and resurrection of Jesus, the foundation of our hope and joy.

Just as God had breathed the breath of life into Adam, so, too, God spoke and the breath of life *reentered* Lazarus's body. Remember, God had formed Adam "from the *dust* of the ground" (Gen. 2:7, emphasis mine). But due to Adam and Eve's rebellion against God, their God-given work had been made challenging and painful. God told Adam,

"You will eat bread by the sweat of your brow
until you return to the ground,
since you were taken from it.
For you are *dust*,
and you will return to *dust*." (Gen. 3:19, CSB, emphasis mine)

Friend, the raising of Lazarus points to the *reversal* of the fall and anticipates new creation. Notice that Jesus didn't just bring new life to Lazarus. He also *reversed* the decay of death and restored Lazarus to physical health and wholeness. And don't you think that's worthy of celebration? Don't you think this God is worth knowing and loving, even if it means walking through the grief of laying down who you hoped he was to know who he truly is?

In one of my favorite children's books on grief, *Goodbye to Goodbyes*, Lauren Chandler imagines that Martha threw a party after Lazarus rose. And why wouldn't she? Her brother had been dead but was now alive! What was once a funeral reception was now a literal celebration of (physical) life party! Mourning and wailing were replaced with dancing, singing, laughter, feasting, rejoicing, and proclamations of praise.

Little did they know that in a short time Jesus himself would be crucified and laid in a sealed tomb. But as Lazarus's story foretold, Jesus' death wasn't the end of the story. The end of the story will be celebration (Rev. 19:1-8).

CELEBRATING LIFE

When celebrating feels near impossible, the reality of who Christ is and what he has done on your behalf can ground you and help you find joy in even the hardest places. Biblical scholars affirm, "Christian joy is no mere gaiety that knows no gloom, but is the result of the triumph of faith over adverse and trying circumstances, which, instead of hindering, actually enhance it."[9] In other words, cultivating genuine joy in places of desolation is nothing short of miraculous, for celebration actually serves to grow our faith in God.

In a letter to an author whose words ministered to my soul, I wrote,

> I laughed out loud as I read your book in NICU room 217b. I laughed not because all is as it should be but because God is still good and there is still joy to be found every day. For example, I experienced surprising joy when my son decided to projectile poop while I was changing his diaper in his Isolette. In an effort to save the cords and machines, I caught it with my hand. And you know what? I was delighted. I was baptized by poop, and in that brief moment, I felt like a real mom who actually got to tend to the needs of her child. It was beautiful!

Celebration in times of sorrow is hard-won, which makes it even more precious. It may not be easy, and it may not be enjoyable initially, but friend, you have reason to celebrate—whatever your circumstances.

- If you are a member of the body of Christ, you have reason to rejoice (see 1 Cor. 12:27).
- If you've seen God's glory and witnessed his majesty, you have reason to worship (see 2 Pet. 1:16).
- If you've tasted and seen that the Lord is good, you have reason to delight in him (Ps. 34:8).

- If you've experienced anything—anything at all—that is good, true, or beautiful, you have reason to thank him (see Phil. 4:8).
- And if, like the disciples, you're still a bit confused about how your specific loss will be redeemed, you still have reason to trust him.

Because, as Jesus informed his disciples, "Our friend Lazarus has fallen asleep, but I'm on my way to wake him up" (John 11:11, CSB). Translation: *Jesus is coming* (Rev. 22:7)! And nothing—not even death—can keep God from accomplishing his purposes. "This is the will of my Father: that everyone who sees the Son and believes in him will have eternal life, and I will raise him up on the last day" (John 6:40, CSB).

An echo of God's proclamation over his good creation (Gen. 1), celebration points to the future (Rev. 21), when all will be as it should be: good and without grief. *Life is worth celebrating.*

REFLECTION QUESTIONS

1. Spend additional time rereading and reflecting on the Scriptures at the beginning of the chapter about God being the God of joy and celebration. How does this truth help you better know God as he really is?

2. To what degree do you consider yourself an active participant in your own healing journey with God? Is this an area in which you'd like to grow?

3. By the power of the Holy Spirit, how might you cultivate eyes to see God's goodness, even in the midst of your pain, which could lead to celebratory joy?

PRAYER

God, I want to know and experience celebratory joy. Thank you that it isn't dependent on my circumstances but based on who you are. Grant me eyes to see you at work. May I be attentive to your will and ways and be an active participant with the Holy Spirit in my own healing journey. Help me live with the end of the story in mind. Amen.

You turned my wailing into dancing;
  you removed my sackcloth and clothed me with joy,
that my heart may sing your praises and not be silent.
  LORD my God, I will praise you forever.

PSALM 30:11-12

10

The One Who Goes Before You: *Trust*

In their fright the women bowed down with their faces to the ground, but the men said to them, "Why do you look for the living among the dead? He is not here; he has risen!"

LUKE 24:5-6

I believe in Christianity as I believe that the Sun has risen, not only because I see it, but because by it I see everything else.

C. S. LEWIS, *THE WEIGHT OF GLORY*

With clinical detachment she informed me that I had caused my unborn child's heart abnormality. Me. His mother. I was the one entrusted with nurturing, nourishing, and protecting my growing son, both inside and outside the womb, but I had failed. I had taken my doctor-prescribed daily antidepressant all through my pregnancy, and now we would all suffer for it. David most of all.

Two months and two hospitals later, I was holding my sleeping son, both of us bound and clipped to his many machines. David's heart and lungs were failing. We had reached the end of all possible medical interventions, so Jason and I were left trying to gulp down a lifetime of memories in just a few hours.

Dr. Sutcliffe was leaving for the day, and he circled back to our room to check on us. How were we handling the news? Did we have any further questions? I nodded at Jason, and he asked Dr. Sutcliffe to step outside the room. David shouldn't have to hear it, and I couldn't bear to hear it again. So Jason bravely asked.

The plan was that Jason would tell me Dr. Sutcliffe's answer when I had the emotional capacity to handle the truth—be it days or years later, or never. *Did I really want to know?* But then Jason walked back in and said that Dr. Sutcliffe wanted to speak with me. Would it be okay if he came back into the room? I nodded.

Dr. Sutcliffe walked back in, quietly pulled a chair up next to me, and sat down. His eyes smiled, and then he gently said, "Tiffany. You didn't do this to David. I'm sorry you were told that your medicine caused his heart abnormality, but it's just not true. The research doesn't support that conclusion." But I protested. I wanted the truth, not the false comfort of someone trying to assuage the guilt of a grieving mother. And so I asked again, twice. And twice I was given the same answer: "You didn't do this."

Both my executioner and my deliverer were pediatric cardiologists. Both had the degrees and experience to back up their claims. The first doctor had spent less than thirty minutes with us. But Dr. Sutcliffe had walked with us through the worst week of David's short life and ministered to our family in ways that I can only describe as God's love made real. He had loved us enough to deliver the news that our baby was no longer a candidate for a heart transplant and then loved us enough to sit and cry with us in the windowless consultation room instead of rushing out to the next patient. If Dr. Sutcliffe had spoken the difficult truth before, why wouldn't he speak the truth now?

And in that moment, I chose to believe him. Why? Because

we knew Dr. Sutcliffe and he intimately knew us. He had proved himself to be credible and trustworthy. And on the day before David died, I received a most precious gift—relief.

* * *

All of life comes down to trust. And the reason you and I are on this grief journey is because God didn't intervene or rescue or show up in the ways we expected him to. Our trust in God was broken, or at the very least, we felt like it had been misplaced, and we were left mourning the God we thought we knew on top of grieving what we'd lost. And so we've each been in relationship counseling with God to see if there is a way forward and if our trust in God can be rebuilt as we get to know him anew.

But as you know, the rebuilding of trust is long, arduous work. It takes time, patience, energy, humility, more patience, and the willingness to enlarge your perspective, temporarily suspend judgment, truly listen, and give the other party the benefit of the doubt. In other words, you first have to extend a bit of trust to even determine whether restoration is possible. And when you've been hurt, that's asking a lot.

Trust is defined as "assured reliance on the character, ability, strength, or truth of someone or something."[1] So it makes sense that trust is often built upon truth and that the lack of truth can erode trust. When pain clouds the way, it's helpful to go back to the truth.

When asked by Pilate why the Jews were accusing him and whether he was indeed their king, Jesus replied, "You say that I am a king. In fact, the reason I was born and came into the world is to *testify to the truth*. Everyone on the side of truth listens to me"

(John 18:37, emphasis mine). To this Pilate retorted, "What is truth?" (John 18:38).

It's said that you can trust the man who died for you, but even renewed trust in Jesus is meaningless if Jesus didn't rise from the dead as he promised (Mark 8:31). The entirety of the Christian faith hangs on what happened next.

NEW AND TRUE

Before the predawn hours of Easter morning—before the inky blackness of night turned to a soft mourning-dove gray that hinted at the brilliance to come—there was a garden.

Not *that* garden. Another garden. John records, "At the place where Jesus was crucified, there was a garden, and in the garden a new tomb, in which no one had ever been laid" (John 19:41).

The first garden had been a beautiful place meant for life, but sin and death had entered it. Adam and Eve were therefore put out of the garden, and angels and a flaming sword prevented humans from entering it again and gaining everlasting life (Gen. 3:24).

The second garden was in a place of death, but new life would spring forth from it. And not even Roman guards (Matt. 28:4) would be able to keep the God-man from exiting the tomb and gifting all believers with everlasting life.

> On the first day of the week, very early in the morning, the women took the spices they had prepared and went to the tomb. They found the stone rolled away from the tomb, but when they entered, they did not find the body of the Lord Jesus. While they were wondering about this, suddenly two men in clothes that gleamed like lightning stood beside them. In their fright the women bowed

> down with their faces to the ground, but the men said to them, "*Why do you look for the living among the dead? He is not here; he has risen!* Remember how he told you, while he was still with you in Galilee: 'The Son of Man must be delivered over to the hands of sinners, be crucified and on the third day be raised again.'" Then they remembered his words. (Luke 24:1-8, emphasis mine)

Each person who encountered the empty tomb on Easter morning came with a particular perspective and reason for being there (Matt. 28:1-10; Mark 16:1-11; Luke 24:1-12, John 20:1-18). Each came with a selective knowledge of Jesus and certain expectations about the role they would play.

Spend some time reading the empty tomb passages above and try to imagine yourself in the scene. Reflect on what you witness and take a few minutes to journal your response below. Which person are you in the Easter morning story, and what brings you to the tomb? What is your relationship with Jesus? What do you expect to experience or do? Whom do you expect to encounter?

Perhaps you came to the tomb expecting to grieve the God you thought you knew only to find his body missing (Luke 24:3).

Perhaps you came to the tomb expecting to prepare your friend's body only to find that your labor of love is no longer needed (Mark 16:1).

Perhaps you came to the tomb expecting a massive boulder to block your path only to find the path already divinely cleared (Mark 16:3-4).

Perhaps you came to the tomb expecting to defend it from attack only to find that the battle is already over (Matt. 28:4).

As we can well imagine, those present at the empty tomb experienced the gamut of emotions as "trembling and astonishment overwhelmed them" (Mark 16:8, CSB). We're told they were "afraid" (Matt. 28:5), "alarmed" (Mark 16:5), "perplexed" (Luke 24:4, CSB), "amazed" (Luke 24:12, CSB), and "filled with joy" (Matt. 28:8) and that at least one of them "wept" (John 20:11). In the midst of their confusion and attempts to comprehend what had happened, the eyewitnesses of the empty tomb experienced both joy and sorrow, mourning and rejoicing. Why? Because God was doing something new and was inviting each of them to further trust him.

> "Forget the former things;
> do not dwell on the past.
> See, I am doing a new thing!
> Now it springs up; do you not perceive it?" (Isa. 43:18-19)

Like those eyewitnesses, you and I are being invited to perceive something new and true: Even in the midst of confusion, mourning, and pain, there can be hope. There can be joyous celebration.

And there can also be renewed trust in the one who goes before us, leading us into resurrection life.

THE RISEN GARDENER

Even after encountering angelic beings glowing with bright light in the empty tomb, Mary Magdalene was still confused as to what had happened to Jesus' body (John 20:11-13). And it's into this state of disorientation that Jesus spoke truth. John records, "She turned around and saw Jesus standing there, but she did not realize that it was Jesus. He asked her, 'Woman, why are you crying? Who is it you are looking for?'" (John 20:14-15).

Jesus invited Mary to truly see and comprehend what was before her. And we've explored many of these same questions together in our respective journeys of loss and restoration:

- "Why are you crying?" *Because I'm grieving the loss of something/someone precious to me.*
- "Who is it you are looking for?" *The real God, whoever he is. I can't find him (John 20:13). Who will help me with the massive burden I'm bearing (Mark 16:3)?*
- "Why do you look for the living among the dead?" (Luke 24:5).

Why indeed? Because Jesus' victory over sin and death (2 Tim. 1:10), his redemption of Israel as well as everyone grafted into the family of God (Eph. 3:6), and his ushering in of the Kingdom of God (Mark 1:15) looked *nothing* like the disciples expected. Even though Jesus had forewarned his disciples about what was to happen (Mark 9:31), there isn't a single "Old Testament verse that has a dying and rising mashiach [Messiah]."[2] It seems some beliefs die hard, even in light of new understanding.

And I know you get that. As you've been on this journey of rediscovering who God truly is, some of your false assumptions about and understandings of God have been challenged. You've been invited to discard the distortions—which is much easier said than done—but what are you to pick up in their place?

Knowing God is a lifelong pursuit that will never be fully accomplished. In fact, we will spend all eternity further knowing, delighting in, and dwelling with our triune God. And honestly, God's plans of redemption and restoration are not always obvious in our lives. While we place our hope in the one who will one day make all sad things come untrue,[3] that day is not now. So there is sometimes confusion. Metaphorically speaking, we sometimes mistake the dead for the living and the living for the dead. But if you hear nothing else, hear this: Keep taking that next step of trust. Keep lamenting, wrestling, and asking the hard questions. Keep going, just like Mary did.

Mary, assuming Jesus to be the gardener, said to him, "Sir, if you have carried him away, tell me where you have put him, and I will get him" (John 20:15). Some speculate that Mary misidentified Jesus because she was standing in the darkened tomb and he was in front of her, face obscured in shadows and backlit by the bright morning light. Or perhaps Mary's eyes were not yet spiritually open, as was the case with the disciples on the road to Emmaus (see Luke 24:31).

Whatever the cause, Jesus revealed his true identity with just one word: "Mary." When he spoke her name, Mary knew that the living God was speaking to her (John 20:16). Jesus had already delivered Mary from demonic oppression (Luke 8:2), and now he had delivered her from eternal separation from the Father. Mary had stepped from darkness into light.

And maybe "the gardener" was the perfect name for Jesus. Because even in places of death and destruction, resurrection life is never far away for a child of God. "In him was life, and that life was the light of all mankind. The light shines in the darkness, and the darkness has not overcome it" (John 1:4-5).

DEATH BEFORE LIFE?

One of the great mysteries of the Christian faith that we must contend with is that death precedes life. When a single seed falls to the ground and dies, it produces many seeds (John 12:24). Jairus's daughter died before being raised to new life (Matt. 9:24-25). Jesus was crucified before he rose on the third day with a glorified body (Luke 24:36-43). And we, too, have experienced a kind of death—death to our old selves (Rom. 6:6). But it is that very death that makes way for new and better life—eternal life with God (Rom. 6:8).

The apostle Paul writes, "We were therefore buried with him through baptism into death in order that, just as Christ was raised from the dead through the glory of the Father, we too may live a new life. For if we have been united with him in a death like his, we will certainly also be united with him in a resurrection like his" (Rom. 6:4-5). In other words, not only is God trustworthy, but because Jesus died and rose again, we shall too!

So we rejoice that we are no longer permanently dust bound; yet we are still a marked people. Our bodies are physical stories told in pimples and stretch marks, scars and birthmarks, calluses and wrinkles.

It is astonishing that the risen God-man forevermore bears a physical, albeit gloried, body. But what is most shocking is that Jesus' body still bears the marks of nails driven into his hands and a spear thrust into his side (John 20:25-28)—the cost of our salvation.

Somehow, in God's economy, scars are no longer tender places of pain but a visual history of God's redemptive work in your life.

My friend, your pain has left a visible scar. You and I both know it. There is no amount of concealer, collagen filler, or skin grafting that can fully remove your scars. The question now is this: Which voice will you allow to speak loudest in your life: your scars of pain, hurt, and disillusionment with God or the one who was "pierced for [your] transgressions" and "crushed for [your] iniquities" (Isa. 53:5)?

Would you be willing to move—even an inch—toward trusting our faithful and true God and believing he can bring something beautiful from your hurt places? For "by his wounds we are healed" (Isa. 53:5).

LOVED TO DEATH

For most of my adolescence, I was consumed with the fear of dying. When you grow up in a church that declares that there is no assurance of salvation, anything related to death and dying is terrifying. After all, the moment of your death is beyond your control, so at all times and in all places you must be in right standing with God and others to attain salvation or else suffer eternal torment.

It was a suffocating burden for my eight-year-old self to bear because there were many things outside my control. Others didn't always like me (which was torture for a people pleaser), I couldn't always make peace with them (which was frustrating for a perfectionist consumed with doing the "right" thing), and if God was as angry and fickle as I understood him to be, pleasing him was a continually moving target.

Even when I was introduced to the God of love and came to understand assurance of salvation for all believers (John 10:28-29; 1 John 5:11-13), my fear of death didn't go away. It merely morphed into something less obvious and slipped undetected into my adulthood as a lie from the enemy. Isn't everyone afraid of dying alone with no one to comfort them and bear witness to their pain?

But about a year after David died, I was shocked to realize that I genuinely no longer feared death or dying. As a grieving mother, I had wanted to know where David was, what he was doing, and what believers had to look forward to after death. So I fervently prayed through and intensely studied Scripture, scholarly commentaries, and academic theology books on life after death (disembodied life in the afterlife; i.e., when believers "go to heaven") as well as life *after* life after death (when we dwell with Jesus in resurrected bodies in the new heaven and new earth).[4]

I discovered that something truly glorious awaits us, and that understanding increased my faith and trust in God. You see, heaven and eternal life weren't very appealing to me when life was going well. I had all that I needed and mostly all that I wanted. But when my son unnaturally preceded me in death, suddenly I was so hungry for the fulfillment of God's Kingdom and to be reunited with David that eternal life became not only beautiful but also real to me.

I now more fully appreciate what awaits me, and most importantly, who awaits me—the God of love: "God is love. Whoever lives in love lives in God, and God in them. This is how love is made complete among us so that we will have confidence on the day of judgment: In this world we are like Jesus. *There is no fear in love. But perfect love drives out fear, because fear has to do with punishment*" (1 John 4:16-18, emphasis mine).

And because of my greater understanding and experience of God's goodness and love, which further increased my ability to trust him and receive his comfort, my fear of death dissipated. Whether tomorrow I am in a car accident that flings my body into an unseen ditch and I die alone or I die of old age in my own home surrounded by loved ones, I know in the depths of my soul that Love will comfort me and bear witness to my pain. I am not alone, and eight-year-old Tiffany wasn't alone either. She may have been unaware of God's loving presence, but that doesn't change the fact that God has always been present with me in my suffering. And nothing, not even death, can separate me from Love:

> Who shall separate us from the love of Christ? Shall trouble or hardship or persecution or famine or nakedness or danger or sword? As it is written:
>
> "For your sake we face death all day long;
> we are considered as sheep to be slaughtered."
>
> No, in all these things we are more than conquerors through him who loved us. For I am convinced that neither death nor life, neither angels nor demons, neither the present nor the future, nor any powers, neither height nor depth, nor anything else in all creation, will be able to separate us from the love of God that is in Christ Jesus our Lord. (Rom. 8:35-39)

So even though it felt like God deserted me in the aftermath of David's death, the scriptural reality that he was with me—even in my most devastating moments—helps me believe that he never left my side.

I now know that God was not absent when David died. And that brings me great comfort (Ps. 23:4).

Journalist Elizabeth Stone suggests that to have a child is to have your heart go walking around outside your body, and that is vulnerable enough, thank you very much. However, when the precious heart outside my body was deemed incompatible with life, my greatest fear was compounded: *David will die alone apart from love.* And be it life or life after death, it's all hell apart from love.

David was so fiercely loved. And he died. And it felt like hell.

But God.

In a journal entry a week after David's death, I wrote,

I don't want to be here.

Dr. V has declared David dead. I didn't see the moment when he passed from life to death, but Jason felt it. How brief and finite life is. With the fertilization of one egg, life sprang forth. And now life is no more. I didn't see either. Would it have helped if I had?

We ask for a quiet moment to be with our son. Strangely, I feel an overwhelming sense of peace, of release. It is over. It is finished. David is no longer suffering. Jason hands David to me, and I play "I Can Only Imagine" while gently swaying around the CVICU room with David. Mommy and baby are dancing. Only he is there, and I am here.

What a glorious day this is for him. He is meeting Jesus face-to-face. No one should have to endure what David suffered. I rejoice that he is no longer suffering. But we are suffering.

APRIL 2018

Honestly, Jason and I still suffer and daily grieve David's absence. But the deepest cry of my heart was answered: My baby boy was not and is not alone.

Love has gone with David where I cannot yet go: to the grave (Ps. 139:8). And because Love went with David to the grave, I know Love will also raise David up to new life one day. And because Love can and will do that, just as he has promised, I can trust God.

Friend, this is the gift of life after death: eyes to see that Love has never left.

REFLECTION QUESTIONS

1. What criteria do you use to determine whether someone or something is trustworthy? Do your criteria reflect that which is good, true, and beautiful? (In other words, faulty criteria lead to a faulty evaluation. Are your criteria accurate?)

2. To what degree does the true God meet your criteria?

3. What might further trusting God in your grief journey look like?

PRAYER

God, I want to trust you more. I wouldn't be on this journey, wrestling with you through the pain, if I didn't desire to believe you are who you say you are. So would you increase my trust in you? When I cannot see, when I don't understand, when I'm blinded by pain, would you remind me of who you are? You are my risen Savior, and you are redeeming my scars. Thank you for being trustworthy and true. Amen.[††]

"Remember, I am with you always, to the end of the age."

MATTHEW 28:20, CSB

†† For an imaginative prayer exercise on desiring to see God, visit tiffanystein.com.

PART 4

life

11

Cultivate Life: *Colaboring with God*

Praise be to the God and Father of our Lord Jesus Christ, the Father of compassion and the God of all comfort, who comforts us in all our troubles, so that we can comfort those in any trouble with the comfort we ourselves receive from God. For just as we share abundantly in the sufferings of Christ, so also our comfort abounds through Christ.

2 CORINTHIANS 1:3-5

"As for us, we cannot help speaking about what we have seen and heard."

ACTS 4:20

It was about six months after David's death, and the topic of bodily resurrection came up in women's Bible study. Alice, our senior pastor's wife, had written a study based on the Apostles' Creed, and it was assumed that she would teach that lesson. But I asked to teach that lesson instead, and Alice graciously stepped aside. Why? Because she sensed that I had something I needed to share.

But it was more than that. My body carried a trauma that needed expressing and now a hope that needed voicing. And so I took the stage and looked around. It was my first time teaching since David had died, and my emotions threatened to undo me. I knew what this message had and would cost me, but it was worth the price. Because they needed to know. My women needed to not just know but *see* that death isn't the end. Life is. And so I preached this: *The best is yet to come.*

The tears flowed, my head ached, and I felt utterly empty after pouring out my soul in message form twice in one day, speaking with dozens of women, receiving their stories of loss, and praying over the grieving.

In God's hands, *God, what do you want from me?* had become more than a question of purpose. It had become an invitation to create something beautiful with him in anticipation of what is to come—*love that knows no loss*. And so I kept on preaching, upheld by the women's prayers and lovingly enveloped in their perfumed arms.

You may not be called to take a stage, but you do have a listening audience. People are watching you and wondering, *How is he still standing? How can she still trust God? How can he sing in worship when God allowed this to happen to his family? How does she have joy in the midst of sorrow?*

The very thing you desperately wish had never happened opens a door for authentic conversations with others about life, death, and the dash in between. And although encouraging, comforting, or pointing someone to Jesus will never undo the pain you've experienced, it can be redemptive to witness God bring beauty from ashes (Isa. 61:3).

PUSH BACK THE DARKNESS

Together we've explored the person and promises of God and been reminded over and over of his steadfast presence. Through death, darkness, and light, he has revealed himself to be the God of *more than*, the God who is more loving, compassionate, and gracious than we ever thought possible. What's more, as twenty-first-century believers who live between the two comings of Christ, we know the cosmic power of Christ's resurrection as well as the hope of Christ's return. Praise God!

But after walking through the scorching fire, what comes next? On my best days, I genuinely desire for God to redeem my suffering for his glory and the good of others. But on my worst days, I covetously attempt to be my own redeemer, a phoenix rising from the flames, proving to all the doubters that what doesn't kill you makes you stronger. Whatever approach you and I may take, we are a people who demand that our suffering be redeemed.

Yet in our attempt to make meaning from what we don't understand and thereby "redeem" the pain, we frequently get it wrong. Consider the disciples after Jesus had risen. Luke records in Acts 1:3-8,

> After his suffering, he presented himself to them and gave many convincing proofs that he was alive. He appeared to them over a period of forty days and spoke about the kingdom of God. On one occasion, while he was eating with them, he gave them this command: "Do not leave Jerusalem, but wait for the gift my Father promised, which you have heard me speak about. For John baptized with water, but in a few days you will be baptized with the Holy Spirit."
>
> Then they gathered around him and asked him, "Lord, are you at this time going to restore the kingdom to Israel?"
>
> He said to them: "It is not for you to know the times or dates the Father has set by his own authority. But you will receive power when the Holy Spirit comes on you; and you will be my witnesses in Jerusalem, and in all Judea and Samaria, and to the ends of the earth."

The disciples had lived all three years of ministry with Jesus in excruciating detail and were still grappling with all that had occurred. In an attempt at meaning making, they asked, "Lord, are you at this time going to restore the kingdom to Israel?" (Acts 1:6). After all they'd suffered, given up, and lost, the restoration of Israel was the only thing that made sense to the disciples.

But Jesus reminded them to focus on what he had already told them in the upper room: "It is for your benefit that I go away, because if I don't go away the Counselor will not come to you. If I go, I will send him to you" (John 16:7, CSB).

So Jesus invited his confused disciples to colabor with him in spreading the gospel. By the empowering of the Spirit, the disciples would go on to courageously share what they had seen and heard, even amid violent persecution (Acts 4:20). Because of this, thousands upon thousands would receive the gift of true life and the disciples would participate in their own healing journey and see the broken pieces of their story redeemed. *They just didn't know it yet.*

If, like the disciples, you're still wondering, *God, what am I to do with* this*: my suffering, my scars, my story? Can you redeem even* this*?* there is good news. For whatever reason, God invites you and me to join him in his redemptive work. He can do it alone, of course, but the God of the universe self-limits in hopes that we will partner with him in doing what we were always meant to do: walk in communion with him and live as his image bearers (Gen. 1–2).

Before the fall, Adam and Eve were truly alive in Christ. They walked with God, spoke with him face-to-face, and as his image bearers on the earth, were delegated with the power and authority to steward all creation according to God's purposes and design. In essence, they were to reflect the Life (John 5:26) by bringing forth life from the womb and from the ground and then creating environments where that life could flourish (Gen. 1:28; 2:15).

The fall was the anti-birth—the decay and decomposition of life collapsing in on itself—*death that leads to darkness.* But Jesus initiated a new birth into the family of God via his living, dying, and rising (John 3:3; 1 Pet. 1:3-4)—*light that leads to life.* And so it makes sense that there would be a recasting, a redeeming, if you will, of the original mandate. Right before his ascension to heaven, Jesus commanded, "Go, therefore, and make disciples of all nations, baptizing them in the name of the Father and of the Son and of the Holy Spirit, teaching them to observe everything I have commanded you. And remember [or *see*], I am with you always, to the end of the age" (Matt. 28:19-20, CSB).

As followers of Jesus, you and I are called to join with the Holy Spirit in propagating life. And part of "preach[ing] the gospel to all creation" (Mark 16:15) and cultivating your specific gifts (1 Cor. 12:7) is stewarding your story.

Full stop. If you just heard the record scratch and are now a bit jumpy, thinking, *How could I ever share my testimony?*, stick with me. You and I have experienced great loss. And what could push back the darkness more than to proclaim the light and life that Jesus has brought *in* your loss?

SHARE YOUR STORY

Friend, there is power in sharing your testimony. In fact, it's so powerful that the testimonies of the saints (that includes you and me!) will be part of defeating the devil and his schemes at the end of the age. We read in Revelation 12:11, "They triumphed over him by the blood of the Lamb and by the word of their testimony."

There are no caveats. The testimonies we are given are not usually stories of victorious overcoming or exceptional faith; rather, our testimonies are about the God who has met us in the darkest moments of our lives. As Henri Nouwen writes in *The Wounded Healer* (emphasis mine):

> Nobody escapes being wounded. We all are wounded people, whether physically, emotionally, mentally, or spiritually. The main question is not "How can we hide our wounds?" so we don't have to be embarrassed, but "*How can we put our woundedness in the service of others?*" When our wounds cease to be a source of shame, and become a source of healing, we have become wounded healers. Jesus is God's wounded healer: through his wounds we are healed. Jesus' suffering and death brought joy and life. His humiliation brought glory; his rejection brought a community of love. *As followers of Jesus we can also allow our wounds to bring healing to others.*[1]

And Paul writes in 2 Corinthians 2:14-16 (CSB), "Thanks be to God, who always leads us in Christ's triumphal procession and through us spreads the aroma of the knowledge of him in every place. For to God we are the fragrance of Christ among those who are being saved and among those who are perishing. To some we are an aroma of death leading to death, but to others, an aroma of life leading to life."

In contrast to the stench of death, you and I are called to be a fragrant aroma of life. Our words and lives are to be so permeated with Christ that before we even arrive the scent of Christ carried on our persons has already permeated the place and diffused the darkness. In other words, you and I are to help lead others to life—not despite our scars but *with* our scars.

So part of what's next for you involves witnessing to God's goodness in your life by telling *your* story. And here's the secret: You don't have to have it all resolved. (And honestly, it won't all be resolved until Jesus returns.) What makes your story appealing and lends you credibility is the very fact that you don't claim to have figured out loss, suffering, or God. But you have lived it, and you're still here—faithfully wrestling, working, and walking with God. And that's truly beautiful. *Can you see the beauty in your story?*

As you process how to share your story, consider organizing it around answering this central question: *How has God sustained me through loss?* Here are a few additional questions to process as you compose and communicate your story.

1. *Before:* What was your life like before the loss? What did your relationship with God look like? How would you have explained God's character to someone else?

2. *During:* What did you lose? (While some details are helpful for understanding what you're walking through, your listener doesn't need to know everything. Too much detail can derail the story and shift the focus to your pain instead of the encouragement you're seeking to offer.)

3. How did that loss challenge and call into question what you thought you knew about God? What was confusing to you about God? What didn't seem to make sense any longer?

4. *After:* Looking back, how has God been present in your suffering, even if you couldn't see him at first? How has

he sustained you and shown you his comfort, goodness, and love?

5. *Now:* What does your relationship with God look like now? What do you understand about God and yourself that you didn't know before? What lingering questions do you have, and what are you continuing to wrestle with? (Your story is ever evolving as you grow and learn, and ultimately, your story is still being redeemed.)

6. If you could encourage someone walking through a similar loss who is also questioning or wrestling with God, what would you say?

Here a few tips for sharing your story:

- Remember that the main character of the story isn't you but God. Keep the focus on him and his faithfulness to you.
- Vary your story according to whomever you're communicating with and their specific needs. Consider how much time you have to share, how long you'll be able to keep their attention, what they might need to hear in particular, their pain points, their current understanding of God, the context in which you're sharing, your relationship with them, and so on.
- Know that it's okay if you get emotional. You're emotional because there is both joy and sorrow and your life has forever changed. However, if telling any particular part of your story causes you to sob uncontrollably, have a panic attack, become depressed, or otherwise exhibit distressing

behavior, wait to share that part until you've metabolized your loss a bit more.

- Remember that you are not in charge of the audience's response. Your role is to share as you're prompted by the Holy Spirit. Their response is between them and God, and fruit cannot be manufactured. It is a gift and work of the Spirit (1 Cor. 3:6-7).

- Keep in mind that you are not God's defense attorney. You don't need to defend, explain, or argue on behalf of God's person or character. This is not an argument to be won but an opportunity to share about your personal encounter with God. After all, logical proofs can be debated or dismissed, but it's hard for your listener to dismiss or explain away hope and new growth in your life when you've just walked through painful loss.

- You can trust that God will give you the words when the time comes and will fill you with confidence, conviction, and boldness. Pray ahead of time, as the disciples did, *Lord, enable your servant to speak your word with great boldness* (see Acts 4:29).

LIVE YOUR STORY

After Jesus issued the great commission, he ascended into heaven to be with the Father. We read in Acts 1:9-12, 14:

> After he said this, he was taken up before their very eyes, and a cloud hid him from their sight.
>
> They were looking intently up into the sky as he was going, when suddenly two men dressed in white stood

> beside them. "Men of Galilee," they said, "why do you stand here looking into the sky? This same Jesus, who has been taken from you into heaven, will come back in the same way you have seen him go into heaven."
>
> Then the apostles returned to Jerusalem from the hill called the Mount of Olives, a Sabbath day's walk from the city. . . . They all joined together constantly in prayer, along with the women and Mary the mother of Jesus, and with his brothers.

For anyone who has ever been given instructions and told "Go!" but still stared ahead blankly and then asked, "What?": This scene is for you, my four-year-old, and the fourth graders I teach. And okay—me, too.

But I don't think the disciples had tuned out Jesus and were lost in daydreams of ruling Jerusalem with thrones on his right and left sides. I think they were awestruck and speechless with wonder. They were finally seeing—*truly seeing*—Jesus, and now he was gone. So they kept staring. Perhaps he would return again?

Reminiscent of the question "Why do you look for the living among the dead?" (Luke 24:5) asked after Jesus had risen from the tomb, the angels asked the disciples, "Why do you stand here looking into the sky?" (Acts 1:11). In other words: *Jesus is not here anymore. Now go. Cultivate life!*

And go they did. The disciples returned to Jerusalem, were united in prayer, and received the Holy Spirit, and the church was born (Acts 1–2).

So what does it mean to not just share your story but live it? The disciples' behavior gives us an example. Still threatened by the disruption Jesus had caused to their coveted way of life, the religious leaders immediately persecuted and arrested the disciples.

Luke records, "When [the religious leaders] observed the boldness of Peter and John and realized that they were uneducated and untrained men, *they were amazed and recognized that they had been with Jesus*" (Acts 4:13, CSB, emphasis mine).

Don't miss this. The disciples themselves had neither accomplished anything nor possessed anything to suggest that they would become influential leaders in a worldwide movement. They were "uneducated and untrained." They were from small, unimportant towns. They were common laborers living everyday, ordinary lives—they were the everyman, the everywoman. But then they met Jesus. And everything changed. Now the disciples were boldly preaching and living out the reality of the resurrection. These divinely appointed disrupters of the status quo were inviting others to partake in resurrection life.

In other words, purpose and meaning can be formed from your suffering not only by you sharing your story but by you actually going and living out your new story. And if you want to be recognized as someone who has been with Jesus, you actually have to be *with Jesus*. After all, if you've walked with Jesus through the fire and have the scars to prove it, shouldn't your life now attest to that reality? Shouldn't others be able to recognize that you've *been with* Jesus and *are still walking* with him now (Eph. 5:8-10)?

* * *

Mark's sudden death was shocking and tragic in a way that I still can't seem to wrap my mind around, but I don't feel abandoned by God this time. Instead, God has given me eyes to see his good and loving presence in this season of mourning, and I feel sustained by him.

MAY 2024

Over the years since David's death, God has permitted me glimpses of his redemptive work. I rejoice that a woman visiting Bible study came to faith when she witnessed the outpouring of prayer on our family's behalf. Others came to faith when a pastor shared our testimony during his sermon. Jason and I have been able to speak uniquely to the circumstances surrounding infant loss and to comfort bereaved parents. Emma Ruth, at age three, could articulate her hope in the resurrection, when she will see Papa (Mark) again and finally get to meet David.

But as strange as it sounds, the most redemptive experience yet was getting to walk with Jason's family—my family—through Mark's hospital stay and subsequent death. Why was it redemptive? Because in real time I was sharing the comfort I had received from God with Mark, Jill (my mother-in-law), Jason, and Megan (2 Cor. 1:3-4) while simultaneously reliving David's life and death through renewed eyes that granted me an enlarged perspective. I marveled that it was my very suffering that equipped me to be useful in this situation and to be to my family what others had been to me: the corporeal community of God.

Others had sacrificially walked with me through death and back, and now I had the honor and privilege of passing on that gift to my family. It was a call I answered with joy, but not because I enjoyed the hospital or seeing my loved ones suffer. No one enjoys that. Being physically alive in the presence of death is the sharpest contradiction of all.

No, it was a joy because I got to partner with God in alleviating some of my family's suffering, one cup of ice chips at a time; and through this, a bit of the Kingdom crashed into ICU room 317. And I'd like to think that David was honored and Jesus smiled.

REFLECTION QUESTIONS

1. As you reflect not just on your journey through loss but on the entirety of your life, in what ways has God invited you to be a "wounded healer"?

2. Once you've composed and written out your story, who might God be inviting you to share it with? Pray that God will grant you discernment to see those in need of his comfort.

3. Scott Erickson writes, "Our woundedness [can be a] surprising avenue of holy transformation."[2] In what ways might God be using your suffering as an avenue of holy transformation in your life and in those around you?

PRAYER

God, thank you for bringing purpose from my pain. I don't understand it—and it certainly doesn't make the deep pain of loss worth it to me—but thank you for not wasting my pain. Use me as you see fit. I want to continue to receive your comfort and pass on that comfort to others. May my sharing and living of my story help bring healing to the hurting, myself included, and bring you glory. Amen.

No, we neither make nor save ourselves. God does both the making and saving. He creates each of us by Christ Jesus to join him in the work he does, the good work he has gotten ready for us to do, work we had better be doing.

EPHESIANS 2:10, MSG

12

The One Who Dwells with You: *Life Everlasting*

"Therefore my heart is glad and my tongue rejoices;
my body also will rest in hope,
because you will not abandon me to the realm of the dead,
you will not let your holy one see decay.
You have made known to me the paths of life;
you will fill me with joy in your presence."

ACTS 2:26-28

"If I go and prepare a place for you, I will come back and take you to be with me that you also may be where I am. You know the way to the place where I am going."

JOHN 14:3-4

There are moments in life that take your breath away. Because when heaven and earth converge, what can you do but stand in awe of resplendent beauty plunging into inconsolable suffering? For a fleeting moment there is neither life nor death nor even time, for Love has consumed all else. These are the thin places treasured in my heart, glimpses of the inbreaking Kingdom.

DECEMBER 2024

David made heaven real to me. But Emma Ruth made the return of Christ an imminent reality in our household.

One of my deepest longings is for David to be remembered and not forgotten. In a redemptive thread that I never could have imagined nor contrived, that desire is partially fulfilled in my daughter. Born two and a half years after her brother, Emma Ruth never met David. Yet because Emma Ruth brings David into the present as she looks toward the future, David has become a real person to her. Family memories are still made with David because of my intentionality to remember him and incorporate him into family traditions and Emma Ruth's capacity to imagine a future beyond what she can see.

Before David was born, my dad gave David a book called *Grandpa and I* and inscribed on the first page a loving note about how he looked forward to their many adventures together. Emma Ruth cherishes the book and takes the inscription literally. Still learning about sharing (aren't we all?), she frequently tells me, "When Jesus returns and David is alive again, I'm going to give David back his book and read it to him. I think he'll really like it!" The second return of Christ is as real and imminent to her as waiting until after lunch to receive her coveted fruit snacks. It is a given, and it is wonderful.

And now with the loss of Mark, we talk about Papa all the time. Just yesterday she "read" to me a card she had decorated with colorful marker scribbles: "Dear Papa, I hope you're alive again soon." Emma Ruth gets it. Death steals life. But Jesus is victorious over the grave. And one day soon, Jesus will return and destroy "all dominion, authority and power. . . . The last enemy to be destroyed is death" (1 Cor. 15:24, 26), and then we will all be raised—*to life everlasting.*

HE WILL COME AGAIN

If everlasting life doesn't stir your heart's affections, perhaps it's because you've never truly grasped all that awaits you as a child of God.

Many of us have been sold a bill of goods declaring that eternity with God will be some sort of disembodied existence where all we do is either pursue our own pleasures devoid of any purpose (eternal golf games, anyone?) or lie prostrate before the throne singing hymns with all the enthusiasm of a robot. Neither of these is a true, appealing, or compelling vision to build your life around.

Others of us haven't bothered to think much about the specifics, since our eternal destination is secure. Yet your view of the future informs your today because, consciously or unconsciously, you live with a specific end in mind. Your understanding of how the story ultimately ends shapes how you live within your own story. So what end do you have in mind? And most importantly, is it true?

What Scripture says about the end times is admittedly vague and open to interpretation, but this we know: Christ will come again, the dead will be raised in resurrected bodies, and all will stand before the judgment seat of Christ. Those who know God will dwell with him forever in the new heaven and new earth, and those who do not know God will spend all eternity apart from him.

God described to Isaiah the events surrounding Christ's second coming this way:

> "See, I will create
> new heavens and a new earth.
> The former things will not be remembered,
> nor will they come to mind.
> But be glad and rejoice forever
> in what I will create,

> for I will create Jerusalem to be a delight
> and its people a joy.
> I will rejoice over Jerusalem
> and take delight in my people;
> the sound of weeping and of crying
> will be heard in it no more." (Isa. 65:17-19)

And to the apostle John, God revealed a vision of the new creation:

> Then I saw "a new heaven and a new earth," for the first heaven and the first earth had passed away, and there was no longer any sea. I saw the Holy City, the new Jerusalem, coming down out of heaven from God, prepared as a bride beautifully dressed for her husband. And I heard a loud voice from the throne saying, "Look! God's dwelling place is now among the people, and he will dwell with them. They will be his people, and God himself will be with them and be their God. 'He will wipe every tear from their eyes. There will be no more death' or mourning or crying or pain, for the old order of things has passed away." (Rev. 21:1-4)

Friend, this is the reality we look forward to! In this beautiful marriage of the new heaven and new earth, *all* that is lost and broken will be restored, redeemed, and recreated. Crying will be replaced with rejoicing, loneliness will be replaced with familial belonging, and death will be replaced with everlasting life.

But that's not all. John continues:

> He who was seated on the throne said, "I am making everything new!" Then he said, "Write this down, for these words are trustworthy and true."

> He said to me: "It is done. I am the Alpha and the Omega, the Beginning and the End. *To the thirsty I will give water without cost from the spring of the water of life.* Those who are victorious will inherit all this, and I will be their God and they will be my children." (Rev. 21:5-7, emphasis mine)

There is coming a day when *all* your longings and desires will find their perfect fulfillment in Christ. Those unanswered questions? Those lingering doubts? Those pain points that no amount of counseling or medication can fix? That disease that remains incurable? That loved one who dwells in hopelessness? That relationship that appears irreconcilable? That dream that was quashed? All those missed moments and opportunities? They will *all* be redeemed. Your thirst will be so slaked by living water that you will never thirst again (John 4:14; 7:37-39).

And at last, on that great day, you and I will see and know God face-to-face (1 Cor. 13:12). Not as we wish him to be, but as he is—good, true, and beautiful. *And somehow you and I will be even more beautiful for having suffered and endured* (see James 1:12).

REFLECTION QUESTIONS

For this exercise, try to set aside the contexts in which you've heard this passage previously read, as well as whatever you envision heaven or life everlasting to be like. Pray that you will have ears to hear this passage afresh and simply allow the beauty of 1 Corinthians 13:4-13 to inform your understanding of what everlasting life with God will be like.

> Love is patient, love is kind. It does not envy, it does not boast, it is not proud. It does not dishonor others, it is not

self-seeking, it is not easily angered, it keeps no record of wrongs. Love does not delight in evil but rejoices with the truth. It always protects, always trusts, always hopes, always perseveres.

Love never fails. But where there are prophecies, they will cease; where there are tongues, they will be stilled; where there is knowledge, it will pass away. For we know in part and we prophesy in part, but when completeness comes, what is in part disappears. When I was a child, I talked like a child, I thought like a child, I reasoned like a child. When I became a man, I put the ways of childhood behind me. For now we see only a reflection as in a mirror; then we shall see face to face. Now I know in part; then I shall know fully, even as I am fully known.

And now these three remain: faith, hope and love. But the greatest of these is love.

1. Read this passage through a second time, substituting *God* for *love* and *he* for *it* in verses 4-8 ("God is patient, God is kind . . ."), since "God is love" (1 John 4:8). How is God described?

2. Why does love never fail nor end (1 Cor. 13:8, ESV)?

3. What is partial or incomplete right now, as we await Christ's second coming?

4. The NIV translates the first part of verse 10 as "when completeness comes," and the ESV reads, "when the perfect comes." Who or what is verse 10 referencing?

5. What do believers have to look forward to when Christ returns?

6. Why is love the greatest spiritual gift? What role do you think love will play in the new heaven and new earth?

PRAYER

God, you are Love, and I long for the day when I will see and know you face-to-face. I confess that I still don't understand why you allowed so much suffering in my life, but I thank you for the redemption and beauty you are bringing from it. Grant me an eternal mindset, and when I doubt your goodness, remind me that I'm still living in the messy middle and that the story is not yet finished. For you are the God who makes all things new, and you have led me back to Life (see Ps. 119:50). Amen.

What no eye has seen, no ear has heard,
and no human heart has conceived—
God has prepared these things for those who love him.
1 CORINTHIANS 2:9, CSB

EPILOGUE

Found

If you were to use one word to sum up your entire faith story thus far, what would it be? *Believing*, *hopeful*, *trusting*, or *persevering*? What about *questioning*, *waiting*, or *searching*?

When you think of the apostle Thomas's faith story, you might label it *doubting*. But doubt didn't characterize Thomas's entire walk with Jesus. In fact, long before doubt was attached to his name, Thomas was characterized as a bold, logical leader.

When the disciples tried to persuade Jesus to avoid returning to Bethany to raise Lazarus, it was Thomas who rallied the others and "said to his fellow disciples, 'Let's go too so that we may die with him'" (John 11:16, CSB). And when Jesus declared that he was going away to prepare a place for them and that his disciples knew the way to where he was going, it was Thomas who forthrightly responded, "Lord, . . . we don't know where you're going. How can we know the way?" (John 14:3-5, CSB).

What's interesting is that both these interactions were intricately tied to belief (John 11:15; 14:1). In each interaction Jesus issued a statement of belief, Thomas responded, and Jesus in turn revealed even greater things, which further increased Thomas's trust in God. It seems that for having grappled with God, Thomas was gifted a fuller understanding of God.

Which brings us to a defining moment in Thomas's life. Jesus had risen from the grave that morning, but he had not yet appeared to all his disciples:

> When it was evening on that first day of the week, the disciples were gathered together with the doors locked because they feared the Jews. Jesus came, stood among them, and said to them, "Peace be with you."
>
> Having said this, he showed them his hands and his side. So the disciples rejoiced when they saw the Lord.
>
> Jesus said to them again, "Peace be with you. As the Father has sent me, I also send you." After saying this, he breathed on them and said, "Receive the Holy Spirit. If you forgive the sins of any, they are forgiven them; if you retain the sins of any, they are retained."
>
> But Thomas (called "Twin"), one of the Twelve, was not with them when Jesus came. So the other disciples were telling him, "We've seen the Lord!"
>
> But he said to them, "If I don't see the mark of the nails in his hands, put my finger into the mark of the nails, and put my hand into his side, I will never believe." (John 20:19-25, CSB)

And friend, in our own darkest moment and questions, we were Thomas. You were Thomas. I was Thomas. We knew God, but then traumatic loss occurred, and the devastation we experienced seemed incongruent with God's character. And so we wrestled.

In grief and disappointment, I declared that if God didn't show up in my Dark Night, then he wasn't the loving God I believed him to be. In pain and disillusionment, you may have challenged God's sovereignty, questioned his goodness, doubted his mercy, or cast aside his grace. Like Thomas, you may have made such a specific demand of God that you were certain your ultimatum would never—could never—be met.

But here's the thing about Thomas missing Jesus the first time: It ultimately served to draw him further into fellowship with Christ. He may have missed Jesus once, but he certainly wasn't going to miss Jesus a second time. And so *Thomas lingered.* He lingered around the people and places of God, hoping to get a glimpse of his risen Lord.[1]

You, too, have lingered, my friend, and accepted the invitation to be drawn further into fellowship with Christ. Although burdened by uncertainty, you chose to do the hard work of excavating your grief and inviting God—the true God—to meet you there. You've been on a journey, and like Thomas with his fellow disciples, you've been anxiously awaiting an encounter with Jesus.

We're not told why Jesus delayed a week in revealing himself to Thomas. And ultimately, *why* he delayed doesn't matter. What matters is that Jesus came for Thomas.

John continues in John 20:26-29:

> A week later his disciples were in the house again, and Thomas was with them. Though the doors were locked,

> Jesus came and stood among them and said, "Peace be with you!" Then he said to Thomas, "Put your finger here; see my hands. Reach out your hand and put it into my side. Stop doubting and believe."
>
> Thomas said to him, "My Lord and my God!"
>
> Then Jesus told him, "Because you have seen me, you have believed; blessed are those who have not seen and yet have believed."

Neither physical walls nor the walls of Thomas's locked heart could keep Jesus out. Instead, in his time and according to his plan, Jesus met Thomas with profound and specific love. Notice that Jesus didn't rebuke Thomas for his doubt, nor did Thomas have to deliver his demands to Jesus' face. Jesus already knew. And so Jesus simply gave Thomas what he needed to believe—permission to touch his scars: "By his wounds we are healed" (Isa. 53:5).

We don't know if Thomas actually touched Jesus' glorified body, but what Jesus gave, a fuller revelation of himself, was enough to warrant a proclamation of faith and praise: "My Lord and my God!" (John 20:28).

Dear friend, have no fear that by a certain milestone or after a specific calendar date your journey—of mourning the God you thought you knew and of coming to know more fully the living God—must reach its conclusion. You will always be journeying with God. Comfort and assurance come in knowing that he who stormed the gates of hell also knows the locked places of your heart—places you may not even be aware of. God knows exactly what you need to believe, and just as he did for Thomas, he will find you there.

HE IS HERE WITH ME

Just one month before David was born, I wrote this for my church's weekly newsletter:

> Psalm 23. It's one of the most familiar and widely memorized of the Psalms. It's read at funerals, framed and hung in living rooms, memorized in Sunday school, and printed on T-shirts.
>
> And because it's so familiar, I've become somewhat blasé to it. Something known and comfortable, but not really something I cherished or thought much about—until recently.
>
> You see, Jason and I are expecting our first child in March, and so that the baby can grow accustomed to Jason's voice, Jason reads a bedtime story to him at night. The first book Jason read to us was a rendition of Psalm 23 called *Found*, written by Sally Lloyd-Jones and told from the perspective of a little lamb. It begins, "God is my Shepherd. And I am his little lamb."[2] It proceeds to show pictures of Jesus—the Good Shepherd—holding, feeding, going after, and guiding the little lamb.
>
> I bawled as Jason read it, not just because I was overcome by God's extravagant love for our son and experiencing crazy pregnancy hormones, but because the realization hit me that I, too, am that little lamb. I'm loved like that by my Good Shepherd. He holds me, feeds me, goes after me, and guides me. And such tender and compassionate love overwhelms me. It seems too good to be true. I feel unworthy. Yes, God can love Jason, Baby Stein,

and you that way—but me? He couldn't possibly love me like that.

But as Jason and I reread that story to ourselves (and to our son), the truth becomes clearer and plants itself more fully in my heart. God not only *can* love me like that. *He already does* . . .

In providential comfort, God gave us *Found* before we needed it. We read it almost daily to David, both in the womb and in the NICU, and it was read by our pastor at David's funeral. David was buried by a statue of Jesus holding a lamb, a profound and powerful image of God's love for his children. The first two lines of *Found* are engraved on David's tombstone, illustrations from the book hung in Emma Ruth's nursery, and my tattoo is a visual rendering of Psalm 23.

Seven years later, by the grace of God, I can look back and affirm:

Even when I walk through the dark, scary, lonely places . . .
I won't be afraid.
Because my Shepherd knows where I am.
He is here with me. . . .
Wherever I go, I know . . .
God's Never Stopping
Never Giving Up
Unbreaking
Always and Forever Love
will go, too![3]

I feared that I had lost God after David died, but in reality, the true God was revealing himself as the one in whom I am found (Phil. 3:9). For while I was mourning the God I thought I knew, lamenting my sorrows, and bemoaning my undoing, God was gently at work, revealing himself to be the God who weeps with me in my pain and comforts me in my sorrow. He is the mourning God—the God who comes near.

You may not yet see him, but God is present and working on your behalf nonetheless: "Blessed are those who have not seen and yet have believed" (John 20:29).

Blessed are those who are grieving, confused, hurt, struggling to understand, and disappointed in God.

Blessed are those who, in faith, continue to wrestle with God and sit in the pain of lament.

Blessed are those who cry out to the only God who ever hung upon a tree, "My God, my God, why have you forsaken me?" (Matt. 27:46).

Blessed are those who hit the Wall and witness their own deaths.

Blessed are those who persevere in the Dark Night and become attuned to the sound of silence.

Blessed are those who wait with expectant—and sometimes agonizing—hope for the light revealed in the darkness.

Blessed are those who can't fully comprehend—yet still receive—God's promise: "I am the resurrection and the life" (John 11:25).

Blessed are those who live at the junction of joy and sorrow, choosing to courageously persist in love, even when it hurts.

Blessed are those who practice subversive joy and declare in the face of death that life is worth celebrating.

Blessed are those who entrust themselves and their loves to Love, who declares, "I am with you always, to the very end of the age" (Matt. 28:20).

Blessed are those who, as wounded healers, push back darkness by living and sharing their stories.

Blessed are those who continue to linger and are rewarded with knowing the God who is so much bigger and more loving, more powerful, and more good than they ever dared to imagine.

Blessed are you, dear friend. For in your grief, you have discovered the God who comes near.

May you walk forward in your foundness, confident in the Good Shepherd, who carries you close to his heart.

> He tends his flock like a shepherd:
>   He gathers the lambs in his arms
> and carries them close to his heart;
>   he gently leads those that have young.

ISAIAH 40:11

Recommended Resources

BOOKS

- *Heaven* by Randy Alcorn
- *Everything Happens for a Reason: And Other Lies I've Loved* by Kate Bowler
- *It's Not Fair: Learning to Love the Life You Didn't Choose* by Melanie Dale
- *Remember God* by Annie F. Downs
- *Embodied Hope: A Theological Meditation on Pain and Suffering* by Kelly M. Kapic
- *Walking with God Through Pain and Suffering* by Timothy Keller
- *Every Moment Holy II: Death, Grief, and Hope* by Douglas Kaine McKelvey
- *And Still She Laughs: Defiant Joy in the Depths of Suffering* by Kate Merrick
- *Getting Grief Right: Finding Your Story of Love in the Sorrow of Loss* by Patrick O'Malley with Tim Madigan
- *Gentle and Lowly: The Heart of Christ for Sinners and Sufferers* by Dane Ortlund

- *Emotionally Healthy Spirituality: It's Impossible to Be Spiritually Mature While Remaining Emotionally Immature* by Peter Scazzero
- *A Grace Disguised: How the Soul Grows Through Loss* by Jerry Sittser
- *Can You Just Sit with Me? Healthy Grieving for the Losses of Life* by Natasha Smith
- *Even After Everything: The Spiritual Practice of Knowing the Risks and Loving Anyway* by Stephanie Duncan Smith
- *It's Not Supposed to Be This Way: Finding Unexpected Strength When Disappointments Leave You Shattered* by Lysa TerKeurst
- *The Deepest Place: Suffering and the Formation of Hope* by Curt Thompson
- *The Soul of Desire: Discovering the Neuroscience of Longing, Beauty, and Community* by Curt Thompson
- *Dark Clouds, Deep Mercy: Discovering the Grace of Lament* by Mark Vroegop
- *Prayer in the Night: For Those Who Work or Watch or Weep* by Tish Harrison Warren
- *Lament for a Son* by Nicholas Wolterstorff

SUPPORT GROUPS

- GriefShare: griefshare.org
- Hope Mommies: hopemommies.org

NEED HELP IMMEDIATELY?

Suicidal thoughts can carry deep feelings of shame and secrecy, which only further the desire to isolate and hide. Please know that you are loved and are worthy of love. You don't need to hide. There is help and hope for you.

If you need immediate help, please call 988 or visit 988lifeline.org. The 988 Suicide & Crisis Lifeline provides 24/7 free and confidential support for people in distress, prevention and crisis resources, and best practices for professionals in the United States and its territories.

Acknowledgments

Jason: There would be no book without you. Thank you for seeing what I saw as a season of loss and confusion as a spacious opportunity for me to sit down with God to write. You are my greatest champion and the one my soul loves. Thank you for your faithful love, which held our marriage together when David died and dares me to go big, especially when I feel small.

Emma Ruth: Thank you for allowing Mommy the time and space to write this book and for being patient with me when I once again had to work when you just wanted to play together. Thank you for all the hugs, cards, flowers, and words of encouragement and for being excited that Mommy's book will one day be "real" (i.e., available on Amazon). 😊 You, sweet girl, bring sunshine wherever you go.

Mama and Daddy: Thank you for instilling in me a love for reading and giving me every opportunity and encouragement to write. You've always believed I've had something to say. Thank you for celebrating every milestone on this long journey to publishing with me, watching Emma Ruth over long weekends so that I could write, and living alongside me through all the highs and lows depicted in this book. Your steadfast love has always been an anchor in my life.

Tamara Royer: There is no better friend than a sister, and you are my dearest friend. Thank you for providing your perspective as a professional counselor for this book and for carrying me through the darkest days of my life. I rejoice that we get to do life together and raise our girls alongside one another.

Jill, the Mankes, the Charlots, Grandma Sue, the Cartwrights, and Mamaw: In many ways, this is your story too. You loved David, held us through it all, and have walked through grief, pain, and suffering of your own. Your personal wrestlings have been a faithful witness to me of what it means to seek God in the dark and trust in his goodness. How blessed I am to have a family that is united before Christ, lives with the hope of the resurrection, and loves unfailingly.

Kat Armstrong: When you officially become a literary agent, I'm counting myself as your first client. Thank you for introducing me to Caitlyn, demystifying the publishing process, coaching me along the way, sharing the tips and tricks of the trade, providing feedback, helping me create a marketing plan, and reminding me that before the birth of anything there are labor pains. But more than that, thank you for being my dear friend of almost two decades and teaching me about the suffering love of God.

Amy Aupperlee: Thank you for staring death in the face and refusing to blink. You journeyed with us to the grave and back and have taught me so much about living with both joy and sorrow and about celebrating who God created me to be. You've seen me at my worst and still love me. Thank you, dear friend, for loving our family as your own.

My readers: Thank you to Kat Armstrong, Amy Aupperlee, Lauren Geppert, Mary Graham, Alice McQuitty, and Kristen Pool, who served as my early readers. Your feedback, suggestions, theological insights, and nuanced questions greatly improved the manuscript. A very special thanks to Sherene Joseph Rajadurai and Tamara Royer, who painstakingly pored over every single word and journeyed with me through it all. Your emails and comments represented sacrificial love to me.

Jenni Swink: When I first met you over chips and salsa eight years ago, I could have never imagined what a beautiful friendship would develop. Thank you for being my spiritual director and accompanying me before, during, and after David. Thank you for holding space for me, lamenting with me, rejoicing with me, and remembering my journey with God even when I forget parts of it. Your ability to remember and call to mind God's faithfulness, especially in the Dark Night, continues to be such a gift. Thank you for being present with me through it all.

Sherry Allen: Thank you for seeing my grief, pain, and fear and meeting me in that stuck place. I'll never forget our first session, when I sat on the carpeted floor of your office and became undone. Cooper laid his head in my lap, and instead of saying something, you simply left your chair and came and sat on the floor next to me. You wrapped your arm around me and held me as I sobbed uncontrollably. That tangible experience of love was the beginning of so much healing work God did in our counseling sessions together. Thank you for being a vessel of his love.

The Well Austin: Thank you to my moms' Bible study friends, CG members, and others who have kindly asked about the progress of this book and faithfully prayed for me for the past three years.

Caitlyn Carlson: I can't believe you picked me! Thank you for believing in this message and championing it every step of the way. You possess the discernment to see what something can be and the skill to bring it to fruition. Thank you for partnering with me in stewarding this message and making it a beautiful one.

Dr. Barry Jones: You taught me the power of being present in the waiting room. Thank you for camping out in the NICU waiting room for two months and making sure we had a pastor, friend, theologian, and fellow sufferer to accompany us through it all. I know the comfort and truth you extended to us were hard-won, and when I think of a shepherd, I think of you.

Sharon Mankin: Thank you for your generous hospitality in allowing Jason and me the use of your lake house during our healing process. It was a beautiful place of refuge, and God met us there in tangible ways. Little did I know that some of the journal entries written there over the following year would be the beginnings of this book.

NavPress and Tyndale House teams: Thank you for collaborating with me on this project. Your skills and expertise have made this book an offering of hope to those who are mourning.

About the Author

Tiffany Stein is an ordained pastor and trusted shepherd with more than a decade of ministry experience. She currently serves as a fourth-grade teacher at Austin Classical School and previously served as the women's pastor and marriage and care director at Irving Bible Church in Dallas, Texas. Tiffany is a native Texan and a graduate of Dallas Theological Seminary and Oklahoma Baptist University. Tiffany has a deep desire to see individuals grow in the fullness and joy of Christ. She comes alive when writing and teaching, delights in one-on-one conversations with a cup of hot tea in hand, and takes every opportunity to hike the Texas Hill Country. Tiffany is married to Jason, the executive pastor at The Well Austin Community Church. They have two beloved children: David, who is with the Lord, and Emma Ruth. The Steins live in the suburbs of Austin.

Notes

DEDICATION

1. Sally Lloyd-Jones, *Found: Psalm 23* (ZonderKidz, 2017), 20.

INTRODUCTION | LOSING GOD

1. "Christ Is Risen," track 11 on Matt Maher, *Alive Again*, Provident Label Group, 2009.
2. "Christ Is Risen."
3. Barry Jones, "Does My Doubt Invalidate My Faith?," sermon, Irving Bible Church, June 14, 2020, Irving, TX, YouTube, 14:43, https://www.youtube.com/watch?v=v2p7Txz_EjE.
4. I would love to learn and hear from you. To receive parts of someone else's story is a sacred honor and something I take seriously. If you feel led to share with me, I promise to treasure what you share and to hold it in love. You can contact me at tiffanystein.com.
5. Peter Scazzero, *Emotionally Healthy Spirituality: It's Impossible to Be Spiritually Mature While Remaining Emotionally Immature* (Zondervan, 2017), 119. Scazzero continues, "What makes this so difficult is how much we invested of our lives into a certain way of following Jesus, into certain applications of biblical truths, only to realize much of it was foolishness or perhaps even wrong. We feel betrayed by a church tradition, a leader, or even God himself. We realize God truly is much larger and more incomprehensible than we thought."

1 | DEATH CAN GO TO HELL

1. While it is not the aim of this book to address theodicy, I highly recommend Timothy Keller's *Walking with God Through Pain and Suffering* (Penguin Books, 2013) as an accessible and nuanced resource if you want to further explore this question. Keller writes with pastoral warmth, keen scriptural insight, and the intellect and breadth required in dealing with such an existential topic.

2. Keller, *Walking with God Through Pain and Suffering*, 208–13.
3. Forgiveness does not mean staying in an abusive situation or relationship. You can forgive someone for hurting you without condoning their behavior. Boundaries are both healthy and necessary, and sometimes that means you cannot continue a relationship.
4. We all know that feelings aren't facts. But feelings are important and do tell us something about what we're experiencing. I'm not suggesting that God literally abandoned me in my suffering. I'm only saying that I felt abandoned and thus had to reckon with the tension of knowing something to be true but not feeling like it was true in that season.

2 | LET IT ALL OUT

1. Soong-Chan Rah, *Prophetic Lament: A Call for Justice in Troubled Times* (InterVarsity Press, 2015), 22.
2. Patrick O'Malley with Tim Madigan, *Getting Grief Right: Finding Your Story of Love in the Sorrow of Loss* (Sounds True, 2017), 70.
3. I love how Katherine Schafler puts this: "While you're alive, do you want to be 'not depressed,' or do you want to feel joy?" Katherine Morgan Schafler, *The Perfectionist's Guide to Losing Control: A Path to Peace and Power* (Portfolio/Penguin Books, 2023), 262.
4. Dane Ortlund, *Gentle and Lowly: The Heart of Christ for Sinners and Sufferers* (Crossway, 2020), 46. Emphasis mine.
5. "In many Hebrew manuscripts Psalms 42 and 43 constitute one psalm." NIV footnote, Psalms 42:1; 43:1.
6. Mark Vroegop, "The 4 Basics of Lament," Crossway, July 14, 2020, https://www.crossway.org/articles/the-4-basics-of-lament.
7. Mark Vroegop, *Weep with Me: How Lament Opens a Door for Racial Reconciliation* (Crossway, 2020), 39.
8. Alice McQuitty, *Draw Near: Experiencing Intimacy with God Through Prayer* (Irving Bible Church, 2020), 37. McQuitty continues, "What God has promised, he will fulfill. It follows then that when we pray for God to fulfill a promise, we can be sure that prayer will be answered. A caution though: It may not be fulfilled in the way we expect it to be or in our timing."
9. Timothy Keller, *Walking with God Through Pain and Suffering* (Penguin Books, 2013), 321.
10. Vroegop, *Weep with Me*, 40.
11. John D. Barry et al., eds., *Lexham Bible Dictionary* (Lexham Press, 2016), under "Heman, Son of Joel."
12. D. A. Carson, ed., *NIV Biblical Theology Study Bible: Follow God's Redemptive Plan as It Unfolds Throughout Scripture* (Zondervan, 2018), 980.
13. Carson, *NIV Biblical Theology Study Bible*, 980.

14. John D. Barry et al., *Faithlife Study Bible* (Lexham Press, 2016), under "Introduction to Lamentations."
15. Barry et al., *Faithlife Study Bible*, under "Introduction to Lamentations."
16. Carson, *NIV Biblical Theology Study Bible*, 1392.
17. Barry et al., *Faithlife Study Bible*, under "Psalm 88:13-18."

3 | THE ONE WHO DIED FOR YOU

1. I'm forever grateful for those precious members of Irving Bible Church who kept giving me a reason to get out of bed and face another day. Their love, prayers, and hope sustained Jason and me.
2. Special thanks to Tamara Royer for reading this chapter and suggesting the addition of this graphic.
3. Dane Ortlund, *Gentle and Lowly: The Heart of Christ for Sinners and Sufferers* (Crossway, 2020), 146.
4. Ortlund, *Gentle and Lowly*, 147. Emphasis mine.
5. Victor P. Hamilton, *Exodus: An Exegetical Commentary* (Baker Academic, 2011), 576.
6. Ortlund, *Gentle and Lowly*, 148.
7. Scholar Douglas Stuart writes, "God will continue his covenant blessings to his people indefinitely—to thousands of generations, not merely thousands of people—as long as they do not break his covenant and thereby force him to unleash its sanctions." Douglas K. Stuart, *The New American Commentary*, vol. 2, *Exodus* (B&H, 2006), 716.
8. Sally Lloyd-Jones, *Found: Psalm 23* (ZonderKidz, 2017), 20.
9. Russ Ramsey, *The Passion of the King of Glory* (InterVarsity Press, 2018), 206.
10. R. T. France, *Tyndale New Testament Commentaries*, vol. 1, *Matthew: An Introduction and Commentary* (InterVarsity Press, 1985), 398. Respected scholars continue to debate the meaning of Matthew 27:46 and whether Jesus was *actually* forsaken by the Father or just *felt* forsaken by the Father. While it seems unlikely that the perfect fellowship of the Trinity was broken on the cross, it seems plausible that, being fully human, Jesus did experience some sort of separation from the Father.
11. France, *Matthew*, 398.
12. Craig A. Evans, *The Bible Knowledge Background Commentary: Matthew–Luke*, Bible Knowledge Series, eds. Craig A. Evans and Craig A. Bubeck (David C Cook, 2003), 514.

4 | BREAKING POINT

1. Janet O. Hagberg and Robert A. Guelich, *The Critical Journey: Stages in the Life of Faith*, 2nd ed. (Sheffield Publishing Company, 2005), 93. For more information on the Wall and the six stages of faith, see the rest of *The Critical*

Journey. Peter Scazzero also offers a brief summation of their work in *Emotionally Healthy Spirituality: It's Impossible to Be Spiritually Mature While Remaining Emotionally Immature* (Zondervan, 2017).

2. Hagberg and Guelich, *The Critical Journey*, 97.
3. Elisabeth Elliot, "The Supremacy of Christ," *Elizabeth Elliot Newsletter*, March/April 1993, https://elisabethelliot.org/resource-library/devotionals/the-supremacy-of-christ-2.
4. C. S. Lewis, *The Last Battle* (HarperTrophy, 2000), 197.

5 | HOLD ON

1. Peter Scazzero, *Emotionally Healthy Spirituality: It's Impossible to Be Spiritually Mature While Remaining Emotionally Immature* (Zondervan, 2017), 103.

6 | LOOK FOR GOD'S GOODNESS

1. Can God raise people from the dead? Absolutely! Is it his normative practice in this day and age? No.
2. *Merriam-Webster Dictionary*, "hope," accessed June 6, 2025, https://www.merriam-webster.com/dictionary/hope.
3. John Mark Comer, "Advent: Hope," *Preaching Today*, accessed June 6, 2025, https://www.preachingtoday.com/sermons/sermons/2021/november/advent-hope.html.
4. Comer, "Advent: Hope."
5. Curt Thompson, *The Deepest Place: Suffering and the Formation of Hope* (Zondervan, 2023), 5.
6. Tiffany Stein, *Expectant Hope: An Advent Devotional* (Wheat & Honey, 2020), 18.
7. Thompson, *The Deepest Place*, xiii.
8. For a robust exploration of Romans 5:1-5 and the relationship between suffering and the formation of hope, see Thompson, *The Deepest Place*.
9. Thompson, *The Deepest Place*, 185.
10. Joshua M. Greever, *Lexham Bible Dictionary*, eds. John D. Barry et al. (Lexham Press, 2016), under "peace."
11. Thompson, *The Deepest Place*, 185.
12. Thompson, *The Deepest Place*, 83.
13. Anne Lamott, *Bird by Bird: Some Instructions on Writing and Life* (Anchor Books, 1995), xxiii.

7 | THE ONE WHO SPEAKS WITH YOU

1. The canon of Scripture is closed, and I'm not implying that God's direction in your life—his "speaking" to you—is on par with or an enhancement of the inspired Word of God. The Word of God is superior, final, and authoritative in all things. Rather, I'm suggesting that when God doesn't

appear to be speaking or seems far away you remember, return to, and find encouragement in the truth God has already spoken in the Bible.

2. Janet O. Hagberg and Robert A. Guelich, *The Critical Journey: Stages in the Life of Faith*, 2nd ed. (Sheffield Publishing Company, 2005), 233.
3. *ESV Study Bible* (Crossway Bibles, 2008), 1887.
4. Robby Galatty, "The Forgotten Jesus Part 2: Was Jesus a Carpenter or a Stonemason?," Lifeway Leadership, April 4, 2017, https://leadership.lifeway.com/2017/04/04/the-forgotten-jesus-part-2-was-jesus-a-carpenter-or-a-stonemason.
5. W. H. Bellinger Jr., "Presence of God," in Archie England et al., eds., *Holman Illustrated Bible Dictionary* (Holman Bible Publishers, 2003), 1326.
6. Mike Livingstone, "The 3 P's of God's Presence," Lifeway, December 3, 2018, https://explorethebible.lifeway.com/uncategorized/the-3-ps-of-gods-presence-session-2-genesis-2810-22. Emphasis mine.
7. "What is the difference between the manifest presence of the Holy Spirit and God's omnipresence?," Got Questions Ministries, accessed June 6, 2025, https://www.gotquestions.org/manifest-presence.html.
8. Bellinger, "Presence of God," 1326–27.
9. Jonathan Petersen, "Advent Is a Time to Recognize the Wonder of God with Us: An Interview with Scott Erickson," Bible Gateway, October 20, 2020, https://www.biblegateway.com/blog/2020/10/advent-is-a-time-to-recognize-the-wonder-of-god-with-us-an-interview-with-scott-erickson.
10. Some names we've been given, some we've chosen for ourselves, and some have been stuck to us against our will. Some of us are carrying around names that need to be discarded and destroyed because not only are they untrue but they're also lies from the enemy meant to keep us trapped in shame. No matter what names you were given or have taken on, God has spoken a greater and truer name over you: Beloved (1 John 3:1-2, ESV).

8 | SUFFERING LOVE

1. Dallas Willard, *The Divine Conspiracy: Rediscovering Our Hidden Life in God* (HarperSanFrancisco, 1998), 11.
2. Tiffany Stein (@tiffany.stein.31), "The misconception about grief," Facebook, April 14, 2023, https://www.facebook.com/tiffany.stein.31/posts/pfbid02BTg9XGHRkUFR8t48adQ15fzQQHs9rTvA2PeHu9FS9kxmSZTYuoJ5XZfYg2Ugho83l.
3. Rev. Dr. Andrew Grosso, "The Bright Sadness: A New Understanding of How the Sorrow of Lent and the Joy of Easter are Inextricably Linked," *The Archangel*, St. Michael and All Angels Episcopal Church, spring 2022, https://issuu.com/smaadallas/docs/aa_spring_final_print/s/14478940.
4. John D. Barry et al., *Faithlife Study Bible* (Lexham Press, 2016), 776.

9 | DARE TO DELIGHT

1. Dallas Willard, *The Spirit of the Disciplines: Understanding How God Changes Lives* (HarperCollins, 1991), 179.
2. Martin H. Manser, *Zondervan Dictionary of Bible Themes: The Accessible and Comprehensive Tool for Topical Studies* (Martin Manser, 2009), under "Joy of God."
3. Willard, *Spirit of the Disciplines*, 179.
4. Karina Kreminski, "Practicing the Discipline of 'Thin Slices of Joy' in 2017," Missio Alliance, January 9, 2017, https://www.missioalliance.org/practicing-discipline-thin-slices-joy-2017.
5. Richard J. Foster, *Celebration of Discipline: The Path to Spiritual Growth* (HarperOne, 2018), 193. Emphasis mine.
6. Andreas J. Köstenberger, *John*, Baker Exegetical Commentary on the New Testament (Baker Academic, 2004), 339.
7. Eugene E. Carpenter and Philip W. Comfort, *Holman Treasury of Key Bible Words: 200 Greek and 200 Hebrew Words Defined and Explained* (Broadman & Holman, 2000), 176.
8. Carl E. De Vries, *The Wycliffe Bible Encyclopedia*, Charles F. Pfeiffer et al., eds. (Moody, 1975), under "embalm," 524–25.
9. D. Miall Edwards, *The International Standard Bible Encyclopedia*, ed. James Orr (Howard-Severance, 1915), 1755, under "joy." See, per Edwards, Acts 5:41; Rom. 5:3; James 1:2, 12; 5:11; 1 Pet. 4:13.

10 | THE ONE WHO GOES BEFORE YOU

1. *Merriam-Webster Dictionary*, "trust," accessed June 6, 2025, https://www.merriam-webster.com/dictionary/trust.
2. Michael S. Heiser, *The Unseen Realm: Recovering the Supernatural Worldview of the Bible* (Lexham Press, 2015), 225–26.
3. Phrasing borrowed from Tolkien's character Samwise Gamgee: "Is everything sad going to come untrue?" J. R. R. Tolkien, *The Return of the King*, collector's ed. (William Morrow, 2022), 951.
4. N. T. Wright has an illuminating book on life after life after death: *Surprised by Hope: Rethinking Heaven, the Resurrection, and the Mission of the Church* (HarperOne, 2018).

11 | CULTIVATE LIFE

1. Henri J. M. Nouwen, *The Wounded Healer: Ministry in Contemporary Society* (Image Books/Doubleday, 1972), 99.
2. Scott Erickson, "Becoming Wounded Healers: Some Thoughts on Resurrection and If It Has Anything to Do with Today," *Image Pilgrimage with Scott Erickson* (blog), May 13, 2025, https://scotterickson.substack.com/p/becoming-wounded-healers.

EPILOGUE | FOUND

1. The idea of Thomas lingering around the people and places of God came from my pastor's 2023 Easter sermon: Tory Mayo, "Linger," sermon, The Well Austin Community Church, April 9, 2023, Austin, TX , https://www.youtube.com/watch?v=joBIlmhh6Zs.
2. Sally Lloyd-Jones, *Found: Psalm 23* (ZonderKidz, 2017), 1.
3. Lloyd-Jones, *Found: Psalm 23*, 9–12, 17–20.